15 NOV '66 C S

DEC '66 N B

DATE DUE

W9-DFW-372

THE

JAMES SPRUNT STUDIES

IN HISTORY

AND POLITICAL SCIENCE

*Published under the Direction of
the Departments of History and Political Science
of The University of North Carolina at Chapel Hill*

VOLUME 47

———————————— * ————————————

Editors

FLETCHER M. GREEN, CHAIRMAN

KEENER C. FRAZER

J. CARLYLE SITTERSON

GEORGE V. TAYLOR

FEDERICO G. GIL

LEGAL ASPECTS OF CONSCRIPTION AND EXEMPTION IN NORTH CAROLINA 1861-1865

By

Memory F. Mitchell

CHAPEL HILL

*

THE UNIVERSITY OF NORTH CAROLINA PRESS

1965

Copyright © 1965 by
The University of North Carolina Press
Library of Congress Catalog Card Number 65-64848
Manufactured in the United States of America

Printed by The Seeman Printery, Durham, N. C.

KFN
7478
.D7
M58
1965

K

M/682
4 4

Ba 23-66

S.B.
1

To Mitch

PREFACE

This study was undertaken almost by accident. The State Department of Archives and History, in 1958, began the tremendous task of microfilming the original case records of the North Carolina Supreme Court. Dating back to the late 1700's, the cases were tied in bundles; they had been untouched for years and had accumulated layers of dust. When the records were opened, it was discovered that the original documents had been rolled together rather carelessly and in many instances several cases had been filed and subsequently tied together. Many of these multiple records were marked with only one case name. To straighten the material and put it in a suitable form for microfilming required review by someone with legal training. It was for this reason that I began working on these records.

When I reached cases from the years of the Civil War, I began to find more and more decisions interpreting the conscription and exemption acts. My interest was aroused and I determined to delve into the question. Research resulted in a wealth of material in the original manuscript records of the Supreme Court, in the printed Supreme Court reports, in newspapers, and in legal materials of North Carolina's government and of the Confederacy.

Realizing that there was more material than could be used in an article, I asked Dr. Fletcher M. Green for advice as to possible use of the study. He suggested that I submit it for the consideration of the editors of the *James Sprunt Studies.* I wish to acknowledge the help which Dr. Green has given me in this instance as well as in the past. The staffs of the State Department of Archives and History, the State Library, and the Southern Historical Collection made materials available to me and were co-operative throughout the months that I did research. I particularly want to acknowledge the assistance of Mrs. Violet W. Quay in reading proof with me. My aunt, Dr. Mary Lynch Johnson, and my husband, Thornton W. Mitchell, read the manuscript and made greatly appreciated suggestions. Thanks to my husband's help in doing last-minute checking of doubtful points, in proofreading, and in making time available to me by sharing the responsibilities of caring for our new twin sons, this study was completed on schedule.

Memory F. Mitchell

Raleigh, N.C.
July 1, 1965

CONTENTS

LEGAL ASPECTS OF CONSCRIPTION
AND EXEMPTION IN
NORTH CAROLINA
1861-1865

I

THE ENACTMENT OF CONSCRIPTION AND EXEMPTION LAWS

Many Southerners, born and bred to a philosophy of the Civil War which accepts as fact the idea that all Confederate boys rushed into the conflict with the enthusiasm displayed by Scarlett O'Hara's friends in *Gone with the Wind*, have not delved deeply into the records of the period. Some Southerners have accepted the suggestion that there may have been a few boys who paid substitutes to go in their stead, but these "isolated cases" are easily explained by their patriotic descendants who offer reasonable excuses for such action. Countless novels, articles, and books have been written on the Civil War, but little attention has been paid to those whose enthusiasm for military service was less than ardent. It is true that desertion and problems of conscription have been studied,[1] but the legal interpretation and application of the conscription and exemption laws has been a subject treated only superficially.

The North Carolina General Assembly enacted laws providing troops for the Confederacy and men for the militia and home guard units. The Confederate States of America passed conscription laws which affected vitally the lives of men of military age after government officials and legislators realized that the ranks could not be filled and maintained with volunteers. The trend of the war itself can be ascertained merely by a reading of the statutes of the Confederate Congress. Conscription acts of April and September, 1862, amendments in 1863, and the drastic changes made in 1864 are reflective of the crises faced by the South at the times of the Congressional enactments.

Despite the need for soldiers, the Confederate Congress never failed to provide for the exemption of many classes of citizens. Not only did the laws permit the use of substitutes, but numbers of professional and skilled workers escaped military service through the operation of the exemption acts. Even the stringent law of February, 1864, continued the system which enabled numerous classes of people to avoid military duty.

The application of the conscription and exemption laws to individual situations resulted in constant disagreement between the military authorities and the civil courts. The number of men who sought discharge

[1] See, for example, Ella Lonn, *Desertion During the Civil War* (New York: The Century Co., c. 1928) ; and Albert Burton Moore, *Conscription and Conflict in the Confederacy* (New York: Hillary House Publishers Ltd. [Reprint of 1924 publication of The Macmillan Company], 1963).

through exemption in its various ramifications was far greater than the average Southerner would dream of, much less know to be fact. North Carolina's courts reviewed the applications for discharge, initiated through petitions for writs of habeas corpus. Chief Justice Richmond M. Pearson, of the Supreme Court, stood as a symbol of freedom to many soldiers who appealed to him for discharge; his decisions caused consternation to both state and Confederate military authorities.

A study of the legal aspects of conscription and exemption must necessarily include a review of the situation which led to the need for the Congressional and state legislative enactments. During the spring months of the year 1861, the atmosphere in North Carolina was filled with evidences of war; but the over-all sentiment indicated a strong Union bias. Activities of Unionist groups were reported in the newspapers, and the Raleigh *Register* actually deferred publication of proceedings of the General Assembly so as to carry full reports of meetings in both towns and counties.[2] The paper told of resolutions passed by groups favoring the Union,[3] and it rejoiced "to see that the lovers of the Union in all parts of the State are thoroughly aroused to a sense of the danger that threatens them. . . ."[4]

On April 17, 1861, a warning was issued to readers of the *North-Carolina Standard*, telling them that reports of war vessels and the beginning of hostilities off Charleston were "totally unfounded . . . [and] furnish a suitable occasion for again cautioning every one to beware of false reports."[5] Considering the fact that the firing at Fort Sumter had occurred on April 12 and that President Lincoln had called for militia three days later,[6] the admonition was slightly belated! Developments in April brought about a reversal in attitude toward the Union. A telegram to Governor John W. Ellis from Lincoln's Secretary of War called for two regiments from North Carolina; the Governor's emphatic reply stated that he could "be no party to this wicked violation of the laws of the country and to the war upon the liberties of a free people. *You can get no troops from North Carolina.*"[7]

Feeling the need for immediate action, Ellis called for a special session of the legislature and suggested that a convention, which could sever the relationship between North Carolina and the United States, be assembled. He commented, "It will require the strength of the united South to drive back the Black Republicans, who, like so many bloodhounds, will be let loose upon the South. . . ." In the same issue

---

[2] Raleigh *Register* (Weekly), February 27, 1861.

[3] *Ibid.*, April 10, 1861.

[4] *Ibid.*, February 27, 1861.

[5] Raleigh *North-Carolina Standard* (Weekly), April 17, 1861. (Hereinafter cited as Raleigh *Standard*.)

[6] J. G. Randall and David Donald, *The Divided Union* (Boston and Toronto: Little, Brown and Company, c. 1961), p. 177.

[7] Raleigh *Register* (Weekly), April 17, 1861.

which reported the Governor's remarks, the Raleigh *Register* gave an account of a meeting in Raleigh at which resolutions were passed condemning the "Black Republican Administration . . . in its folly and wickedness. . . ."[8] In a few short weeks, the newspapers clearly reflected the reversal of sentiment which had taken place in North Carolina.

Even before the action in April, the North Carolina legislators had felt a need to strengthen the law with regard to defense. They had provided that all white males between eighteen and forty-five years of age, except ministers, were to be enrolled in the militia.[9] Legal authority was given for a volunteer corps, with the Governor being empowered to enroll additional men in case of actual war.[10] The legislature also provided for both horse and foot artillery.[11]

Though provision had been made for troops for defense, the truth of the situation of the country was brought home to the people by an order of April 20, 1861, issued by the Adjutant General, instructing volunteer forces to be ready to march on an hour's notice. The Governor directed the Adjutant General to call for the enrollment of thirty thousand volunteers.[12]

With secession a reality in parts of the South, North Carolina was faced with a decision as to her future. At the opening of the special session of the General Assembly in May, Governor Ellis told of federal usurpation of power, of steps taken by the state for defense, and of recommendations with regard to increased military forces.[13] He explained that the time had come for action, saying that "All fraternity of feeling is lost between us and them. . . . There must be a separation at once and forever."[14] He continued his message by congratulating the people on the unity and harmony in North Carolina, adding:

No sooner was it seen that our liberties were menaced by the usurper, than all party feuds were forgotten, and the patriotic fires that burned in the bosoms of our ancestors were rekindled in the breasts of their descendants. The hearts of the people everywhere are prepared for the contest before us.[15]

The Assembly, responding to the Governor's request, authorized him to raise a division or corps of ten thousand men by voluntary enlistment.[16] He was also empowered to ask for and accept twenty

[8] *Ibid.,* April 24, 1861.
[9] *Public Laws of the State of North Carolina,* 1860-1861, c. 24, s. 1. (Hereinafter cited as *N.C. Public Laws.*)
[10] *Ibid.,* c. 24, s. 11.
[11] *Ibid.,* c. 25.
[12] Raleigh *Standard,* April 24, 1861.
[13] North Carolina *Senate Journal* (First Extra Session, 1861), pp. 6-12.
[14] *Ibid.,* p. 13.
[15] *Ibid.,* p. 14.
[16] *N.C. Public Laws,* First Extra Session, 1861, c. 6, s. 1.

thousand volunteers in the militia and to increase the number to fifty thousand if the public exigencies demanded such action.[17] Men who responded to the call were to receive pay and allowances comparable to that of Confederate forces.[18]

Though public opinion had shifted after the events of early April, the legislators evidently did not feel sure enough of their position to open their sessions and debates to all interested persons, for provision was made for secret sessions. Separate journals of the proceedings of these sessions were kept in both the Senate and the House, and members were required to take an additional oath promising not to disclose any of the transactions.[19]

As early as February, the Confederate Provisional Congress had expressed hope that North Carolina would join the seceded states and had indicated its eagerness for the state to "speedily ... unite in our councils, and in such government as shall be formed by these states."[20] Several months passed before the anticipation of Congress was fulfilled. On May 17, Congress voted to admit North Carolina on condition she ratify the Constitution for the Provisional Government of the Confederate States,[21] and three days later the State Convention adopted an ordinance severing the ties between North Carolina and the federal union.[22]

Excitement and exhilaration filled the air of the capital city when news of secession was announced. The ordinance having been anticipated, the Ellis Light Artillery was ready on Capitol Square with six brass field pieces, and its adoption was made known "when the loud-mouthed cannon proclaimed the joyful tidings...." Both the Capitol bell and church bells rang, and the Artillery fired one hundred guns and then "rested a few minutes." Then ten guns were fired; these salutes were followed by three cheers for each of the seceded states and cheers for North Carolina. When the announcement came that the Constitution had been adopted, twenty guns were fired; and the Raleigh *Register* reported the enthusiasm of the crowd as being "beyond our powers of description."[23]

A few days later, the Military Committee of the Convention asked

[17] *Ibid.*, c. 3, s. 1.

[18] *Ibid.*, c. 3, s. 6.

[19] North Carolina *Senate Journal* (First Extra Session, 1861), pp. 28-29, and North Carolina *House Journal* (First Extra Session, 1861), p. 32.

[20] *The Laws of the Confederate States*, Provisional Congress, 1 Sess., February 4-March 16, 1861, Resolution No. 4, passed February 8, 1861. (Hereinafter cited as *Laws of Provisional Congress.*)

[21] *Ibid.*, 2 Sess., April 29-May 21, 1861, c. XXV.

[22] *Ordinances and Resolutions of the State Convention of North Carolina*, 1 Sess., 1861, Ordinance No. 1, ratified May 20, 1861, p. 3. (Hereinafter cited as *Ordinances of the State Convention.*) See also Raleigh *Register* (Weekly), May 22, 1861.

[23] Raleigh *Register* (Weekly), May 22, 1861.

Wesley Jones, a former United States marshall, to determine the number of white males between the ages of eighteen and fifty in the state. He answered by saying such data were not filed in the form requested and that to obtain the statistics "would involve much time and labour. . . ."[24]   About a month later, however, the Convention President learned that the army of North Carolina then consisted of over twenty thousand men, located at twenty-one different posts.[25]   In its same first session, the Convention provided that state troops authorized by acts of the General Assembly should be transferred to the Confederate States of America on the same conditions as if they had been raised under Confederate authority.[26]

When the division between North and South actually came, the question of loyalties was based more on geographical location than on conviction. There were those in the South who sympathized with the Union; there were those in the North who were inclined to agree with the Confederacy. Though most Americans automatically felt attached to their home regions, there were those for whom the decision was difficult. When conscription began, however, officials put men in the army of each section without regard to ideologies.[27]

The matter of loyalty and patriotism was stressed in the spring and summer of 1861 when men were urged to volunteer. Enthusiasm ran high in the months before the drafting of men was begun; and volunteer companies and individuals recruited men by appealing to their emotions and to their devotion to the cause of the South.

As the recruiting campaigns became intense, advertisements in newspapers became more numerous. The Ellis Light Artillery, for example, specified that it wanted none under five feet eight inches in height; it also needed "good strong Horses, from six to nine years of age. . . ."[28]   The conclusion of a report of a volunteer company from Wake County stated that any person wishing "to fight the battles of his country . . . is cordially and earnestly invited to come forward and join the Wake Light Infantry."[29]   Individuals also solicited recruits. One Frank I. Wilson advertised:

I am authorized by the Confederate Government to raise a company of Infantry for the war. I am also assured that such company will be retained

[24] Wesley Jones to Chairman of the Military Committee of the Convention, May 29, 1861, in Secretary of State's Papers, Archives, State Department of Archives and History, Raleigh. (Hereinafter cited as Secretary of State's Papers.)

[25] L. O'B. Branch to Weldon N. Edwards, June 25, 1861, in Secretary of State's Papers.

[26] *Ordinances of the State Convention*, 1 Sess., 1861, Ordinance No. 30, p. 8.

[27] Harold Melvin Hyman, *Era of the Oath: Northern Loyalty Tests During the Civil War and Reconstruction* (Philadelphia: University of Pennsylvania Press, 1954), unnumbered p. ii.

[28] Raleigh *Register* (Weekly), May 1, 1861.

[29] *Ibid.*, July 24, 1861.

in North-Carolina as long as the foot print of an enemy pollutes our soil. . . .
I promise never to give the command of, "Men, go!" but I will say, "Men,
follow!" I shall ask no one to go where I do not lead.[30]

Early efforts to recruit met with enthusiastic response, but by fall
signs of discontent were evident. A newspaper urged the Convention
to reaffirm North Carolina's determination "never under any circumstances to countenance any plan for the reconstruction of the Union.—
We suggest this because there is an impression among the Yankees
that there is a strong Union sentiment in this State. . . ."[31] The impression came in part from the problems connected with recruitment.
One letter explained that "It is hard work to get recruits about town.
There are so many men recruiting. They look like hawks watching a
chicken yard."[32] The importance of keeping the armed forces strong
was stressed by a Raleigh newspaper, and it stated that the knowledge
that military might was being retained at the same or greater strength
was a fact which would "fall heavily upon the Yankee heart . . ." and
would provide "daily evidence that the subjugation of the South is becoming more and more an absurdity, while the impoverishment and ruin
of the North is approaching daily an absolute certainty."[33]

The paper's optimistic statements were reversed less than a month
later when it observed that difficulties should serve to "stimulate us to
more vigorous action. . . ." Civilians were urged to enlist and those in
service were encouraged to re-enlist as a means of carrying out this
policy of "vigorous action."[34]

Governor Ellis, who died in office on July 7, 1861, had been suc-
ceeded by Henry T. Clark.[35] Clark bemoaned the fact that he had "to
rely on an unarmed and undrilled militia for protection . . ." and that a
draft for a third of them had caused great dissatisfaction.[36] In the
midst of his worries about the militia and related problems, Governor
Clark urged enlistment by issuing a proclamation:

North Carolina! Our Country needs your aid for its protection and
defence against an invading foe. The President of the Confederate States

[30] *Ibid.*, October 2, 1861.

[31] *Ibid.*, November 27, 1861.

[32] D. McRae O'Hanlon to Peter Mallett, January 28, 1862, in Peter Mallett
Papers, Southern Historical Collection, University of North Carolina. (Hereinafter cited as Mallett Papers.)

[33] Raleigh *Register* (Semi-Weekly), January 29, 1862.

[34] *Ibid.*, February 19, 1862.

[35] Marshall DeLancey Haywood, "John Willis Ellis," *Biographical History of
North Carolina From Colonial Times to the Present*, 8 volumes. Edited by
Samuel A. Ashe (Greensboro: Charles L. Van Noppen, 1906-1917), VII, 96, 101.

[36] Henry T. Clark to Judah P. Benjamin, February 1, 1862, in R. N. Scott
et al., eds., *The War of the Rebellion: A Compilation of the Official Records of
the Union and Confederate Armies*, 70 volumes in 127 books, atlases, and index
(Washington: Government Printing Office, 1880-1901), Series I, IX, 426. (Hereinafter cited as *Official Records*.)

has made a requisition upon our State to complete her quota of troops in the field. Our own borders are invaded by the enemy in force, now threatening an advance to deprive us of liberty, property, and all that we hold dear as a self-governing and free people. We must resist him at all hazards and by every means in our power.... As you value your rights of self-government and all the blessings of freedom—the hallowed endearments of home and fireside, of family and kindred, I call upon you to rally to their defence, and to sustain the noble and sacred cause to which we are engaged.[37]

Recruitment efforts proving ineffectual, the third session of the State Convention took steps in the spring of 1862 to assure North Carolina's quota of Confederate troops. Provisions were made for the Governor to call for volunteers to meet requisitions for troops, for volunteers to receive credit for time previously served when they re-enlisted, and for the discharge of volunteers after service for three years or sooner in case the war ended before the expiration of the three-year term.[38] Counties furnishing volunteers were asked to complete their quotas by March 15, 1862.[39]

Congress also busied itself with problems of enlistment, working out plans concerning the place of enlistment[40] and the acceptance of volunteers in companies with officers selected by the companies.[41] President Davis was authorized to ask for volunteers, not exceeding 400,000, for a period of not less than twelve months nor more than three years.[42] At its fifth session, in December, 1861, the Provisional Congress authorized the Secretary of War to adopt measures with regard to enlistment and recruitment;[43] a month later, the President was empowered to call on the states for troops to serve for three years or for the duration of the war.[44] Enactments permitted the acceptance of volunteers singly as well as in military units.[45]

The numerous statutes passed by state and Confederate legislators relative to enlistment and recruitment failed to produce the needed results, and rumors of a draft were being heard by the spring of 1862. As early as February, the Greensboro *Patriot* speculated on the question. Saying that Guilford County had done well, the paper continued by stating that

[37] Raleigh *Register* (Semi-Weekly), proclamation of February 22, 1862, in issues of February 26, March 1, and March 5, 1862.

[38] *Ordinances of the State Convention*, 3 Sess., 1862, Ordinance No. 23, s. 1, p. 57.

[39] *Ibid.*, s. 2, p. 57.

[40] *Laws of Provisional Congress*, 2 Sess., April 29-May 21, 1861, c. V, [s. 1].

[41] *Ibid.*, c. V, s. 2.

[42] *Ibid.*, 3 Sess., July 20-August 21, 1861, c. XX.

[43] *Ibid.*, 5 Sess., November 18-February 18, 1862, c. XV.

[44] *Ibid.*, c. L.

[45] *Ibid.*, c. XLVI.

it remains for her to do more. Her full quota of men must be raised, either by voluntary enlistment or by being drafted. We hope her brave sons will not suffer themselves to be *drafted* to maintain and defend every thing dear to them; but that they will rally to the standard of their country's defence, with a determination to conquer the vandal enemy whose foot now pollutes the soil of our State.[46]

The idea of a draft or conscription was traditionally repugnant to the American tradition. The Anglo-Saxon belief in the right of the individual to set his own course of action rather than to be coerced and the conviction that patriotism would motivate him to serve his country meant that there would inevitably be opposition to conscription laws.[47] Actually, there had been conscription as early as the Revolution, but such practice was not common. North Carolina had passed an act to raise men to complete the Continental battalions in May, 1778. The law provided that bounties were to be offered to volunteers, but if a sufficient number did not "turn out" the several companies were to determine which men out of each company of militia should go to make up the quota. Those persons were to be paid bounty in half the amount paid the volunteers, and provision was included that those chosen were to go themselves or "provide able-bodied men to serve in their stead...."[48] A conscription law was considered during the War of 1812, but because of New England opposition and the failure of the two houses of Congress to agree there was no enactment.[49] The idea of conscription for the Confederate army was not, therefore, a new concept.

The *Carolina Watchman*, of Salisbury, reported that South Carolina planned to fill her quota by conscription and that the men who were called would be mustered in for the war. A report that drafted men would not be allowed to choose their officers was regarded by the paper with disfavor; the editor commented that those "who fight our battles ought to be permitted to elect their officers; and to deny this right, and force officers on the men, seems ... to indicate a tendency to standing armies and military despotism."[50]

Another newspaper report stressed difficulties which would ensue from a policy of granting exemptions to specified groups.[51] It was under-

[46] Salisbury *Carolina Watchman*, February 17, 1862, quoting the Greensboro *Patriot*.

[47] James G. Randall, *Constitutional Problems Under Lincoln* (New York and London: D. Appleton and Company, 1926), p. 239. (Hereinafter cited as Randall, *Constitutional Problems*.)

[48] Walter Clark, ed., *The State Records of North Carolina* (Winston, Goldsboro, Raleigh: The State of North Carolina, 16 volumes and 4-volume index [compiled by Stephen B. Weeks for both *Colonial Records* and *State Records*], 1895-1914), XIII, 411-412.

[49] Randall, *Constitutional Problems*, p. 241.

[50] Salisbury *Carolina Watchman*, March 24, 1862.

[51] *Ibid.*, March 31, 1862, quoting the Raleigh *Standard.*

stood that Virginia had passed legislation which exempted one editor, an assistant editor, and other indispensable newspaper employees from military service.[52] Feeling that exemption provisions would inevitably produce dissatisfaction, one editor spoke emphatically, saying:

Exemptions should be made under some fixed and just rule, unbiased by favor or affection. In this State, the law exempts very few, except those who may be pronounced by physicians as unfit for duty, yet the large number who obtain certificates from physicians produce much discontent. People find it difficult to believe that men who until now have been capable of performing any other service, are found to be entirely unfit to make soldiers.[53]

Despite the opposition expressed in the newspapers and the dislike of the idea of conscription on the part of the public, the rumors which had had wide circulation were to prove true and were to take the form of tangible law. Though the Confederate Congress held secret sessions on the subject,[54] reporters from the scene of debate sent out word that a bill to subject every white male between eighteen and thirty-five to military service was under consideration and that "a spirited debate" had occurred in the Senate.[55]

The discussions, debates, and study in the Congress of the Confederate States of America produced significant legislation on April 16, 1862. On that date, the President was authorized to place in military service white male residents of the Confederacy between the ages of eighteen and thirty-five at the time of the call, except in cases of legal exemption. Those already in the Confederate service whose terms were to expire before the end of the war were to be continued in their posts for three years from the date of their original enlistment unless the war should end before that time. Companies were permitted to reorganize and elect officers, and those under eighteen and over thirty-five who were in military units to be reorganized were required to remain in their companies for an additional ninety days except where their places could be filled sooner by other recruits.[56]

Various mechanics were outlined in the law,[57] and a vital issue—the question of exemptions—was settled for the time being. A special provision stated that "persons not liable for duty may be received as substitutes for those who are, under such regulations as may be prescribed by the Secretary of War."[58] Under the terms of the exemption bill, passed

[52] Charlotte *North Carolina Whig*, March 25, 1862.

[53] Salisbury *Carolina Watchman*, March 31, 1862, quoting the Raleigh *Standard*.

[54] Confederate States of America *Senate Journal* (1862), entries for April 5, 7, 8, 9, 10, 11, 16, pp. 114-117, *passim*.

[55] Charlotte *North Carolina Whig*, April 1, 1862.

[56] *Public Laws of the Confederate States*, 1 Cong., 1 Sess., 1862, c. XXXI, s. 1. (Hereinafter cited as *Confederate Laws*.)

[57] *Ibid.*, c. XXXI, ss. 2-8, 10-13.

[58] *Ibid.*, c. XXXI, s. 9.

on April 21, 1862, numerous classes of individuals were excluded from the draft, including those found to be unfit for service; those in the employ of the Confederate states; judicial and executive officers of Confederate and state governments; members of Congress and of state legislatures and their officers; clerks in the government offices; those engaged in carrying the mails; ferrymen on post routes; pilots and others engaged in marine service and in railroad routes of transportation; telegraph operators; ministers engaged in their profession; those working iron mines, furnaces, and foundries; journeymen printers actually printing newspapers; presidents and professors of colleges and academies; teachers having as many as twenty pupils; superintendents of public hospitals, and asylums and nurses and attendants at such institutions; teachers at the institution for the deaf, dumb, and blind; one apothecary in good standing in each apothecary store doing business; and superintendents and operatives in wool and cotton factories who were exempted by the Secretary of War.[59]

The United States Congress was facing the same problems as the Confederacy. The matter of recruitment and the question of conscription were serious on both sides. When the Civil War began, there were three forms of military organization in the country: the regular army, recruited from volunteers, which consisted of appoximately 13,000 men after many Southerners withdrew; an expanded emergency force raised through a system of volunteers agreeing to serve for a limited period of time; and the militia, which was at the same time both a state and federal organization. Though the militia was created by state law with officers appointed by state authority, it was part of the system for national defense though it could also be called for state service. Lincoln's original call for troops, on April 15, 1861, was for 75,000 militiamen. Though about 80,000 were raised under this call, the militia system was inadequate and was hardly more than an organization on paper. Because the militia's organization was left to individual states, many had neglected to make the group the force needed in time of emergency. In his second call, May 3, 1861, President Lincoln asked for volunteers for three years. This call was without legal authorization, though Lincoln expected, and later received, Congressional ratification. By the summer of 1862 the North was faced with the same problems of recruitment as was the South, and Congress enacted a law which was to serve as the basis for conscription on July 17, 1862. Males between eighteen and forty-five were included, and numbers were apportioned among the states by population. Volunteers for this service were to be paid bounties, and and on August 4, 1862, the President ordered a draft of 300,000 militia, with quotas being assigned to the states. The law, which did not expressly provide for conscription, authorized the President to issue regulations, construed to mean the power to order a draft. The provision

[59] *Ibid.*, c. LXXIV.

that the militia was to include all males between specified ages meant, for all practical purposes, military liability.   Thus it might be said that Congress applied the principles of conscription "by the line of least resistance."   Though defects in the old militia system remained, the first step toward full-scale conscription had been laid.[60]

Details regarding the bill passed by the United States Congress are irrelevant to this study, but the fact that both sides in the conflict were faced with similar problems is clear.   The need for manpower, the necessity of personnel for factories and farming operations, the need to provide for those who stayed at home, the resultant confusion and chaos brought about by the abrupt change to a wartime economy were realities on both sides.

To carry out the provisions of the Confederate law, it was necessary to work out mechanics so that those in authority would understand the procedures.   A few days after the exemption bill was passed by the Confederate Congress, detailed regulations of the War Department relative to procedures under the Conscription Act and its application were published in the newspapers.   Those men subject to the draft were given the privilege of volunteering, provided they did so by May 17, and the volunteers would be counted in a state's quota.   Those claiming exemptions were required to make oath to the enrolling officer that they were not subject to draft; after the legal requirements had been met, they were entitled to certificates of exemption.[61]

The drastic measures which Congress had taken caused much talk among the people, and newspapers reflected public opinion.   The *Carolina Watchman* wrote:

We accept and submit to this measure as a necessity for the present time, *"our one great business being, to whip our enemies and save our homes."* We believe the people will accept it on that account as a present necessity. Nevertheless, the people are jealous of their liberties; and so far as our observation goes, they regard this measure with no little apprehension as emanating from that class of men in the South who are on the point of despairing of man's ability to govern himself.   There has been a good deal of loose talk about a monarchy or a Dictatorship, &c., for the South, and it is easy to see how the *plea* of necessity might be employed to accomplish a sudden and radical changee [*sic*] in the form of our government, if indeed, (which we doubt,) there be a party amongst us which desire such a change.   But as the price of liberty is eternal vigilance, and as all encroachments are sure to begin with and emanate from our rulers, we shall take this occasion to warn the people that we are in the very midst of perils, not only from our common enemy, but also from those who we have delegated to transact our public business.   Our National Constitution, cradled, nurtured and perfected in the very arms of war, has, by the conscription, been set aside or over-ridden on the *plea of a war necessity.*

[60] Randall, *Constitutional Problems*, pp. 241-247.
[61] Raleigh *Register* (Semi-Weekly), April 30, 1862.

But yet, the people seem disposed to yield this *inch*—they will do it, because they believe in the *necessity*. But let them look out, henceforth, if our rulers are honest they will not abuse this usurped power. But on the other hand, if an overthrow of our Republican government is the object, and this bill is to be the lever employed for the purpose, you will soon hear of other stern *necessities* still more imperious, and more seriously invading the rights of the States and of the citizen.[62]

The opinion of Randolph Abbott Shotwell was emphatically expressed in the following words:

On the *16th of April* the firm hand was out-stretched to grasp the situation, by the passage of a general Conscription Act, placing the whole country on a war-footing, and requiring every able-bodied citizen—save certain specified exempts—between the ages of 18 and 35 to at once take arms in defense of his section; and of course, compelling those already in the field to remain there. Every male between the ages specified and not exempted for disability or any of the numerous civil offices—was placed at the disposal of the Government—"for three years, or the war"—if the war should outlast three years.

All men in service, *over* or *under*, the given ages were to be held 90 days after the term of their original enlistment expired. A piece of injustice, I think, as it was a poor recompense for their patriotism in volunteering at the beginning of the war, that now after a year of hard service they should be held for three months longer, while those of their age who had been enjoying the comforts of home all this time should be allowed to continue it. But iron-handed necessity demanded that any soldier who could possibly be kept in the field should be kept.[63]

Shotwell explained that men found "all their fond anticipations blasted and years of service before them with very little prospect of one in a dozen of them ever seeing home again unless as a cripple, or diseased wreck of his former self, [which] stirred, as may be imagined, a strong feeling and not a little indignation."[64] The ideas that draftees could select their own officers, were given equal rights with veterans, and were allowed to select their commands and branches of service were appalling to Shotwell.[65] He explained that some companies sought revenge for detention by electing "the most ignorant and idiotic of their comrades to fill the offices . . ."; that he felt as his comrades, "the indignity of being changed, after twelve months of faithful service from the venerable position of 'Volunteers' cheerfully lending their lives and labors to their

[62] Salisbury *Carolina Watchman*, April 28, 1862. The article was copied in the Raleigh *Standard*, May 7, 1862.

[63] J. G. de Roulhac Hamilton and Rebecca Cameron, eds., *The Papers of Randolph Abbott Shotwell*, 3 volumes (Raleigh: The North Carolina Historical Commission, 1929-1936), I, 183. (Hereinafter cited as Hamilton, *Shotwell Papers*.)

[64] *Ibid.*, I, 184.

[65] *Ibid.*, I, 184-185.

country, to the condition of worse than mere hirelings—almost—slaves, —conscripts!" Facing reality, Shotwell concluded by pointing out that he could "understand that the conscript law was an imperative necessity; it must be enforced, or the whole country delivered up to the enemy, and not even the most unappeasable growler was ready to consent to the alternative."[66]

The Raleigh *Register* criticized the position of the *Standard* for saying the only hope for the South was to fight out the war with ranks filled with conscripts and expressing the opinion that the conscript law was to be enforced. The *Register* accused its rival of a change in attitude, believing that it had previously aided the discontents in their thinking and in their efforts to circumvent the law by repeated criticism of the conscription act. The editor remarked that his counterpart on the *Standard* had cried in "his crocodile [*sic*] voice and wept in his paper over the hardship and cruelty of taking men away from their little farms and their crops at this important and critical stage of their culture and preservation." Talk such as that had created opposition to the law and to the officers enforcing it, and the *Register* felt that much dissatisfaction could be attributed to the influence of the *Standard*.[67]

Considering the attitude of the public, it is not surprising to find that those responsible for the execution of the law were faced with numerous problems. Governor Clark wrote to George W. Randolph, Secretary of War, on April 24, saying he desired to carry out the conscription act, but that the late Secretary of War had called on North Carolina for her quota, which was a sixth of the entire white population. He explained that there were about thirty-eight thousand men in the field and that another ten thousand had been recruited. Clark wondered if the state had filled her quota without the necessity of enforcing the conscription act prior to the call for another quota. He also asked whether the additional ten thousand recruits would be counted toward another quota.[68] Randolph replied that the conscription act superseded all calls for quotas; he referred to the regulations which explained the operation of the laws then in effect.[69] To clarify the situation with regard to companies authorized by the Governor prior to the passage of the conscription bill, the Adjutant General ordered the men in such companies to report to Camp Mangum before May 17 (the deadline for the acceptance of volunteers), or they would not be received. The order advised that those not in by the specified time would be subject to the War Department "and had better remain at home till ordered by that Department."[70]

[66] *Ibid.*, I, 186.
[67] Raleigh *Register* (Semi-Weekly), July 30, 1862.
[68] Henry T. Clark to George W. Randolph, April 24, 1862, in *Official Records*, Series IV, I, 1091-1092.
[69] Randolph to Clark, April 30, 1862, in *Official Records*, Series IV, I, 1105.
[70] Raleigh *Register* (Semi-Weekly), April 30, 1862.

Peter Mallett, at the time Major and Assistant Adjutant-General, reported the selection of a good site for a camp of instruction. He stated that returns of sixty-three regiments showed sixteen thousand conscripts, but that the number "will be greatly reduced by exempts and Volunteers since enrolled." His letter continued with a proposal that the state be divided, with a commissioned officer and examining surgeon assigned to each county to enroll conscripts, accept substitutes, examine recruits, and give certificates to exempt persons. Mallett felt that the plan, which had been suggested to him, would save expense in that substitutes would be accepted and certificates given locally rather than at a camp of instruction.[71] Though Governor Clark allowed the use of state officers in the enrollment of conscripts,[72] he declined to order these men to perform the duty. Mallett reported that he had adopted the suggestion made by the Chief Executive to the effect that the patriotism of the officers be relied on; he said the plan had worked well with exception of officers in Johnston County.[73]

The unpopularity of the conscription law did not make the task of the military officials an easy one. Governor Clark expressed his opinion in a letter to Mallett on June 24, 1862, when he wrote:

The Conscript Act is very distasteful to our people and doubts of its constitutionality have been raised and it has only been acquiesced in as a necessity for our welfare. Nevertheless I have rendered it every facility for execution and have used every effort to make it acceptable to our People. For that reason I would carefully avoid all contests about it and I cant [sic] believe the Sec. would sanction the raising of points of dispute or questions of jurisdiction unnecessarily.[74]

Mallett referred to the Governor's sentiments in a letter to the Secretary of War, adding that he disagreed with Clark to some extent and did not believe the law as distasteful as did the Chief Executive. He expressed the belief that it would be necessary to have twenty-five thousand men to fill the regiments to the maximum, but that the estimated number of conscripts was twenty thousand for North Carolina.[75] Mallett may have changed his mind concerning the public attitude, for later, after Zebulon B. Vance became Governor, Vance reported to the Secretary of War that Mallett was having difficulty "in hunting them [conscripts] up." Vance said he had issued an order permitting men to choose regiments if they were not filled, a step which had improved the situation, but Mallett had later received instructions to send all conscripts to specified brigades

[71] Peter Mallett to Samuel Cooper, June 10, 1862, in Mallett Papers.
[72] [Mallett] to Cooper, June 11, 1862, in Mallett Papers.
[73] Mallett to Cooper, July 5, 1862, in Mallett Papers.
[74] Henry T. Clark to Peter Mallett, June 24, 1862, in Mallett Papers.
[75] Peter Mallett to George W. Randolph, June 30, 1863, in Mallett Papers.

without regard to individual wishes.   The result was great dissatisfaction.[76]

The citizens of the mountains were probably more belligerent in their reaction to conscription than those of other parts of the state.   The mountain people had responded well to the early call and the region had sent many of its young men to the army.   The demand for additional troops, when the male population was already depleted, met with opposition.   A writer in Stokes County, for example, stated that thirteen hundred men had already gone and the home folks were suffering deprivations as a result.   Taking conscripts would make it impossible for those at home to support themselves another year.   Two of those in the North Carolina delegation who voted against the bill in Congress were from the western part of the state.   Many westerners felt that the exemption provisions discriminated against the poorer classes and favored those who were rich.[77]

Because of lack of popular support for the conscription bill, the matter of enrollment presented many problems.   Officers who enrolled conscripts were also required to arrest deserters and men who were absent without leave.[78]   In the summer, those liable to conscription under the provision of the act of April 16 were advised not to enlist in any regiment but to report to the commandant of Camp Holmes or be considered deserters.   Officers were notified, by an order issued from Camp Holmes by Major Peter Mallett, not to enlist men liable to conscription.[79]

The cause of enlistment was undoubtedly hindered by such descriptions as the following, carried in the Salem *Press*:

The affecting scenes connected with the departure of Volunteers have given way to the heart-rendering sight of men torn away from their families by the strong arm of the law; heads of families, surrounded by weeping women and children, are forced into the army, their hopes and prospects blighted, if not forever ruined, under the plea of a military necessity, when, it will be remembered that, some eighteen months ago, we were told that secession would be peaceable, and a mere small job to be despatched in the morning before breakfast.[80]

[76] Zebulon B. Vance to George W. Randolph, October 10, 1862, in Frontis W. Johnston, ed., *The Papers of Zebulon Baird Vance, 1843-1862.* (Raleigh: State Department of Archives and History, Vol. I of a projected series, 1963), I, 252-253.   (Hereinafter cited as Johnston, *Vance Papers.*)

[77] John G. Barrett, *The Civil War in North Carolina* (Chapel Hill: The University of North Carolina Press, c. 1963), pp. 183-184.   (Hereinafter cited as Barrett, *The Civil War in N.C.*)

[78] Raleigh *Register* (Semi-Weekly), July 26, 1862.

[79] *Ibid.*, August 6, 1862.   For a discussion of desertion in North Carolina, see Richard Bardolph, "Inconstant Rebels: Desertion of North Carolina Troops in the Civil War," *The North Carolina Historical Review*, XLI (Spring, 1964), 163-189.

[80] Raleigh *Register* (Semi-Weekly), July 26, 1862, quoting the Salem *Press*.

The Raleigh *Register*, after quoting the description, commented that the Salem editor was doing his best to have the law violated when he held up the conscripts as victims of oppression.[81]

Considering the expressed dissatisfaction, it is not surprising to learn that many took advantage of the exemption provisions of the law. The first regulations of the War Department issued after the act of April 16 was passed explained that any person liable to military duty, not mustered into service, who desired to furnish a substitute should report himself and his substitute to a camp of instruction. Provided the substitute was legally exempt, sound and fit for military service, he could be enrolled and the principal discharged. No substitute was to be entitled to transportation or other allowance until he was accepted and enrolled.[82] Various certificates, made on oath, were required—from the substitute and the examining surgeon—before a certificate of exemption was issued to the principal.[83]

Though the problem of enforcement existed both North and South, the law was harder to carry out in the South because of the traditional emphasis on the states' rights philosophy. The lack of uniformity in the plan of conscription in the several states; the ease with which medical exemptions were obtained; the reluctance of some states, notably North Carolina and Georgia, to co-operate with Confederate officials were only three of the reasons for the difficulty.[84] In the North there were disaffected citizens who paid commutation money, misrepresented their ages, feigned sickness and found it relatively easy to obtain an affidavit from a country doctor.[85] Similar tactics were used in North Carolina. Fingers were cut off, skin scaled to produce sores, diseases feigned. One man with dark skin claimed to be part Negro. Family Bible birth records were changed. Some men even worked in the fields, dressed as women.[86]

Administration of conscription was an acute problem throughout the years of the Civil War as military officials on both sides sought to enforce the provisions of the law. Exemptions caused dissatisfaction in the Union and the Confederacy on the part of those unable to be excused from military liability. Numbers of men sent substitutes rather than volunteer even before the conscription act was passed, salving their consciences by paying someone to serve in their stead. The practice was widely accepted throughout the country. In North Carolina, newspaper advertisements for both principals and substitutes appeared frequently. Typical

---

[81] Raleigh *Register* (Semi-Weekly), August 6, 1862.

[82] *Ibid.*, April 30, 1862.

[83] See, for example, certificates in the case of C. F. Lowe, who furnished John McGlocklin as his substitute on November 17, 1862, in Davidson County Miscellaneous County Records, Archives, State Department of Archives and History, Raleigh. (Hereinafter cited as Davidson County Records.)

[84] Spencer Bidwell King, Jr., *Selective Service in North Carolina in World War II* (Chapel Hill: The University of North Carolina Press, 1949), p. 5.

[85] Randall, *Constitutional Problems*, pp. 250-251.

[86] Barrett, *The Civil War in N.C.*, p. 185.

was a notice which was carried in the *Carolina Watchman* for five weeks in April and May, 1862:

Two substitutes, healthy and able-bodied, of good size, over the age of 35 years, are wanted for the war, for which a liberal price will be paid. Apply soon, at this Office.[87]

Another offered five hundred dollars for "a sound able bodied man over 50 years old."[88] A notice in the Raleigh *Register* indicated that a "liberal price" would be paid for a substitute, and the advertisement ended with the thought that a "Citizen of the Confederate States preferred." A prospective applicant was advised to apply to "Conscript" at the *Register* office.[89] In July, 1862, a notice asked for substitutes over thirty-five years of age, with promise of a "liberal price," and the advertisement indicated that the person who inserted it wanted the same words copied, for the conclusion read, "Register copy till forbid."[90]

Similarly, those willing to offer themselves as substitutes also advertised; the payment asked was often high. Two men included details concerning their qualifications:

Two able bodied men offer to serve as Substitutes, free from State or Confederate service, well skilled in military tactics, infantry, artillery, cavalry or broad sword exercises. Willing to serve any where, in any capacity, any company or regiment in the Southern Confederacy, for each, $1200. Address P.O. Box 38, Raleigh, N.C.[91]

Another, an "able bodied substitute, 52 years of age," proclaimed his willingness "to go any where for $3,000."[92] Still another notice informed the public that "Substitutes for the army can be obtained in this section, by paying good prices. Apply to the subscriber, Swift Island, Montgomery, N.C."[93]

The requested prices were generally higher than those actually paid for substitutes. A list delivered to Colonel Peter Mallett at Camp Holmes on December 12, 1862, included the name of the substitute, the name of the principal, and the amount paid. The prices varied from two hundred to seven hundred dollars, with the total for twenty-five men being $10,050. Principals on this list were shown as coming from Randolph, Caswell, Person, Wake, Granville, Chatham, Johnston, Orange, Rockingham, and Alamance counties—an indication of the widespread acceptance of the system.[94] Some payments were lower than the

[87] Salisbury *Carolina Watchman*, April 28, May 5, 12, 19, and 26, 1862.
[88] *Ibid.*, May 5, 12, 19, 26, and June 2, 1862.
[89] Raleigh *Register* (Semi-Weekly), July 23, 1862.
[90] Raleigh *Standard*, July 9, 1862.
[91] *Ibid.*, July 2, 1862.
[92] *Ibid.*, September 10 and 17, 1862.
[93] *Ibid.*, July 16, 1862.
[94] List of Substitute Money Delivered to Colonel Peter Mallett, Commandant at Camp Holmes, December 12, 1862, in Mallett Papers.

$402 average paid for the substitutes on the list furnished to Mallett; in fact, at least one man went as a substitute for payment of only fifty dollars.[95]

With a demand for substitutes, and with men willing to go as substitutes, the next step was probably inevitable. Brokers set themselves up in the business of bringing the two parties together. Even before the draft law was passed, the brokerage business was common in the Richmond area. The system was explained by the newspapers:

> Everything that will pay is snatched at in these times; and we are not surprised to find a number of men in Richmond engaged in the speculations of supply substitutes in the army for those who are to pay for the privilege of staying at home. Regular agencies for this business are advertised in the newspapers, with "splended inducements" and earnest exhortations to "call."—The practice is for the agents to buy up "non-residents," in the shape of Jew pedlers and all sorts of vagabonds, and then to ask twice or three times the price they pay the poor wretch of the customer who is supplied from their office with a substitute. The rates of charges in this disreputable traffic vary, according to the amount of fleecing the customer can stand, and the necessity in which he is placed. We are informed of one instance where a soldier, who was ascertained to have means, and to have been called home on some indispensable occasion, was constrained to pay for a substitute the enormous sum of fifteen hundred dollars.

> This disreputable traffic, which profits on the necessities of certain classes in the community, should at once be terminated by the Government itself taking charge of the whole matter of substitution, and establishing a fixed substitution rate in money, as is the practice in the conscript systems of Europe. The Government could employ the substitute on better terms than the agent, as it would require no commissions or profits for itself; it would protect parties against the exhortations of Shylocks, and against speculations upon their necessities; and it would be enabled, by its direct control of the matter, to keep the practice of substitution under proper guards that it might not degenerate into a system of abuses and corruptions enormously detrimental to the efficiency and spirit of the military service.[96]

The procurement of substitutes through brokers evidently became quite common, for an order of August 1, 1862, forbade the use of agents, indicating that those who acted contrary to the order would be subject to impressment into service. This impressment was to embrace principal, substitute, and agent. There seemed to be some opinion that this order was directed to the Richmond area only,[97] but it could well have applied elsewhere, for the system was known in other areas. A broker in

[95] *In re* Boyden, 60 N.C. 175 (1863).
[96] Raleigh *Register* (Semi-Weekly), March 15, 1862, quoting the Richmond *Examiner*.
[97] Raleigh *Standard*, August 13, 1862.

Raleigh, Frank I. Wilson, advertised in both the *Register* and the *Standard:*

> Persons wishing to engage themselves as Substitutes, and those desiring to employ Substitutes, will do well to call on or address me by letter. Native North Carolinians, over 45 years old, preferred for Substitutes.[98]

It is not surprising that others attempted to profit from the ignorance of their fellow citizens concerning the conscription laws and their application in individual situations. In a notice entitled "Conscription," Thomas Jones & Co. called attention to that firm's willingness to advise prospective draftees on their legal status. The plan was outlined in the following words:

> Thousands in the Confederate States, owing to the different laws and exemption bills passed by the last two sessions of the Confederate States Congress, are so mystified as to their real duties they know not what course to pursue. We advise all who really believe themselves subject to the law to report immediately at the respective camps appointed for the enrollment of conscripts in the different States. To those who believe themselves exempt, we would respectfully say, that on securing our fee, which is FIVE DOLLARS, we will furnish them the law bearing on their cases and every additional information which we have gleaned from the office of the authorities in parallel cases, and we are prepared to take all the responsibility of such advice. We will do nothing but a LEGITIMATE business. Those whom we find are really liable, we will inform accordingly. Those who are not (and there are thousands in every State who are not), we will give them our advice with the law bearing upon their cases.
>
> Having every facility, we are prepared to give every information regarding any other business connected with the army.
>
> Owing to the heavy expense incurred in procuring this information, we will notice no communications unaccompanied with our retaining fee of *Five Dollars.*[99]

Considering the magnitude of the entire operation, the fact that the Confederate States of America was a newly-created government, the attitude of the states toward centralized authority, and public opinion toward the enforcement of the conscription laws, abuses and confusion were to be expected. It was not surprising that there were those who attempted to profit from this chaotic state of affairs, both as to troubled governments and as to perplexed individuals.

The system which permitted exemptions met with criticism, as was evidenced by a meeting of Orange County conscripts. These men, gathered at Camp Holmes, resolved "That we do not approve of that

[98] Raleigh *Register* (Semi-Weekly), September 10 and 14, 1862; Raleigh *Standard*, September 10 and 17, 1862.

[99] Raleigh *Standard*, December 31, 1862.

feature of the act of conscription which tolerates substitutes. In the fight for freedom all should fight, as all will be free."[100] An ordinance introduced in the North Carolina Convention, in April, 1862, would have exempted from military service and omitted from the militia rolls, until others in the militia in the same age group had performed similar military service, those who had furnished a substitute for three years or the war. The fact that this ordinance was laid on the table in May[101] is indicative that North Carolina was not in complete sympathy with the Confederate policy.

The Orange County conscripts, who objected to the system of substitutes, also expressed disapproval of the appointment of one Wayne McDade as deputy sheriff, saying there was little for such an officer to do, "and we look upon it as robbing the army of a good soldier when there is such pressing need for all."[102] Surry County conscripts, holding a similar meeting in early September, 1862, stressed their willingness to serve, but they felt that the law should be enforced impartially. In a resolution, they said they were "mortified to see a portion of our fellow Conscripts, who are equally liable and interested with us, endeavoring to evade the law, by slipping into old forges, ore pits, wood and coal yards; and many of them men too, who one year ago, could not have been induced to go into any of them." The same group continued, saying they thought "it very strange, that certain Post Masters and others, who could perform all the duties of their offices and positions, without aid, up to the time of enrollment, should suddenly find it necessary to appoint one or more assistants and deputies." They expressed dismay at the number of schools which had sprung up, feeling that "the law and justice requires that they should march with us to the battlefield, and leave the old men and ladies to teach the children." Still further, the Surry group regarded "all contractors, manufacturers, and others, who take *Conscripts* into their employment, for the purpose of aiding them to evade the law, as wanting in good faith to the South, and as preferring their own private interest to the public good and safety."[103]

Actually, some employers undoubtedly did try to help those about to be conscripted so that they could stay out of service. An affidavit of the general superintendent of Cedar Falls Company, a Randolph County corporation, verified that ten employees were absolutely essential to its operation of the business of manufacturing cotton yarns and cloth.[104] A newspaper advertisement called for "A good Miller [who] will find

---

[100] *Ibid.*, July 23, 1862.

[101] Records of Constitutional Convention, 1861-1862, in Secretary of State's Papers.

[102] Raleigh *Standard*, July 23, 1862.

[103] *Ibid.*, September 3, 1862.

[104] Affidavit of George Makepeace, July 9, 1862, in Marmaduke Robins Papers, Southern Historical Collection, University of North Carolina. (Hereinafter cited as Robins Papers.)

good employment and good wages, besides exemption from the Conscript Law, by applying at this office."[105]

The fact that the law was not always strictly enforced was well known. Jonathan Worth wrote to Governor Vance, saying there were many in Randolph County who had not reported, but he felt they would do so if they were allowed to join companies of their section. He suggested that the county would have met the draft "manfully" if the men had not been led "to believe that they would be allowed, as far as possible, to select the companies in which they were to serve." He admitted that some would probably have to be taken by force, and that "One great cause of this refusal of our conscripts to enrol themselves in [sic] the exemption of their officers."[106] Vance, in a proclamation of September 18, 1862, urged those using their influence to prevent obedience to the law and those organizing open resistance "to desist from such unpatriotic & criminal conduct: earnestly hoping that all, who are disinclined to defend their homes . . . either by reason of age, infirmity or cowardice will cease to dissuade those, who are willing. . . ." The proclamation concluded with emphasis on the intention of the Governor to enforce the law and a call on "all loyal & patriotic citizens to sustain those who are charged with its execution."[107]

Considering the confusion, discontent, and doubts concerning the conscription act, it was not unexpected when Congress reconsidered its provisions. When the second session of the first Congress convened in August, 1862, President Davis addressed the Senate and the House. He spoke of the acts passed during the previous session to secure the public defense, saying that they had "led to some unexpected criticism that is much to be regretted." He continued by remarking that as a result, the "efficiency of the law has been thus somewhat impaired. . . ."[108] The Raleigh *Register* informed its readers that Congress would again consider the matter of conscription and would probably extend the law to include those between eighteen and forty-five or fifty years of age. The opinion was expressed that "nothing but a conscript law which will force every man capable of bearing arms in the field will accomplish the object."[109]

Confronted with the need for amendments, Congress acted, passing a second conscription act in September, 1862. Newspaper reports on

[105] Salisbury *Carolina Watchman*, October 20, 1862.

[106] Jonathan Worth to Zebulon B. Vance, September 16, 1862, in J. G. de Roulhac Hamilton, ed., *The Correspondence of Jonathan Worth*, 2 volumes (Raleigh: The North Carolina Historical Commission, 1909), I, 187-188. (Hereinafter cited as Hamilton, *Worth Papers*.)

[107] Johnston, *Vance Papers*, I, 191.

[108] Message of President Jefferson Davis to House and Senate, August 18, 1862, in Confederate States of America, *Senate Journal*, 1 Cong., 2 Sess. (1862), p. 227.

[109] Raleigh *Register* (Semi-Weekly), August 20, 1862.

Congressional action of September 4 informed the public of the changes which provided that the President could call white males, not in service and not legally exempted, for three years or the war and could suspend the law where its operation was not politic, using his discretion in this matter. "In the House nothing was done of any interest."[110] Despite the lack of interest in one branch of Congress on that particular day, the entire Congress took a positive step when the new bill became law on September 27, 1862. The draft age was raised to include those between thirty-five and forty-five at the time of the call and not legally exempt. Persons were to be called first to fill companies, battalions, squadrons, and regiments from their own states, and any surplus was to be assigned to organizations formed from each state after passage of the act of April 16.[111] Amendments to the acts of April 16 and September 27 were made in October, with the provision that persons subject to enrollment were to be enlisted whether they were in their state or county of residence or not; when enrolled, they were to be subject to provisions of the law as if they had been in their home territory. The members of military organizations established under state law, while in actual service within the limits of a state, were not subject to the new act.[112]

Instead of discontinuing provisions with regard to exemptions, however, the list was lengthened. Members of the Society of Friends had written the Secretary of War in July, asking if they could be assigned to duties in hospitals. A reply indicated that there would be no objection to Friends enrolled in North Carolina assuming duties "not repugnant to their belief," but that no general order to that effect could be issued. Rather, each case would be decided on its merits.[113] The Society had petitioned the North Carolina Convention in April, 1862, stating its position with regard to war and emphasizing the fact that its principles were of long-standing, which "we cannot yield or compromise in any degree whatever." The Society pointed out that its number in the Confederate states was less than ten thousand, while membership in the North probably exceeded two hundred thousand, that Friends in both sections would take similar positions with regard to military service, and that "We have enlisted under the banner of the Captain of our soul's salvation, Jesus Christ, the Prince of Peace; therefore, in obedience to his express command, we cannot fight, or aid directly or indirectly in any carnal wars."[114] The Convention passed an ordinance exempting members of the Society who produced

[110] *Ibid.*, September 10, 1862.
[111] *Confederate Laws*, 1 Cong., 2 Sess., 1862, c. XV.
[112] *Ibid.*, c. XXXIV.
[113] Raleigh *Standard*, July 30, 1862.
[114] "Memorial," filed with records of Constitutional Convention, 1861-1862, Secretary of State's Papers.

certificates of membership from militia duty and military service, with the proviso that they pay one hundred dollars when called on to do so by the authorities. A further provision was made that those unable to pay were to be detailed to assist in manufacturing salt or to work in hospitals.[115] The Friends were not exempted by the first exemption act of the Confederate Congress, but they, the Mennonists, Nazarenes, and Dunkards were exempted by the law of October 11, 1862. A provision included in the new exemption law required that each one not drafted was to furnish a substitute or pay five hundred dollars into the treasury.[116] A special officer was designated to collect exemption money from members of the sects named in the law.[117]

As was the case in the Confederacy, there was no provision in the Union's Militia Act of 1862 that exemptions be granted because of conscientious scruples. The 1863 law failed to take care of the situation, and there were some cases of genuine suffering on the part of Quakers. The trials of these people resulted in a modification of the law by the United States Congress in 1864, when provision was made for exemption on religious grounds. The similarity in the laws of the two legislative bodies is further shown by the Union's requirement that those exempted for reasons of conscience were to work in hospitals or in caring for freemen or by paying three hundred dollars for the benefit of sick and wounded soldiers.[118]

In addition to the religious groups, the Confederate Congress extended some exemptions and added others in the October, 1862, amendments. Included in the exempted groups were those physically or mentally unfit for service; judicial and executive officers of Confederate and state governments, including postmasters and clerks as allowed by the Postmaster General, but excluding other postmasters, assistants and clerks; state officers declared by their states to be liable to military duty; members of Congress and state legislatures and their officers; clerks in Confederate and state governments, as authorized by law; volunteer troops raised by any state after the passage of the act of April 16, while such troops were in active service under state authority, but not to include any person liable to conscription as a result of the act of April 16; pilots and others in the merchant marine; the president, superintendents, conductors, treasurer, chief clerk, engineers, managers, station agents and masters, two expert hands for each eight miles of track and mechanics actively working for railroad companies, but not to include laborers, porters and messengers; the president, general superintendent and operators of telegraph com-

---

[115] *Ordinances of the State Convention*, 4 Sess., 1862, Ordinance No. 34, p. 85.

[116] *Confederate Laws*, 1 Cong., 2 Sess., 1862, c. XLV, [s. 1].

[117] Edward Needles Wright, *Conscientious Objectors in the Civil War* (New York: A. S. Barnes and Company, Inc., 1961), pp. 105-106.

[118] Randall, *Constitutional Problems*, pp. 260-263.

panies and local superintendent and operators of the companies, not over four in one locality; chief officers, engineers, and mechanics engaged in water navigation; one editor and such employees as the editor might certify to be indispensable for each newspaper; the public printer and those employed to print for state and Confederate governments; ministers engaged in the discharge of their ministerial duties; physicians engaged and having been engaged for the preceding five years in the actual practice of their profession; shoemakers, tanners, blacksmiths, wagon-makers, millers and their engineers, and millwrights engaged in their trade, subject to the condition that the products of their labor be sold at prices not to exceed seventy-five per cent the cost of production or at a maximum fixed by the Secretary of War, and also provided that a violation by any manufacturing firm would mean withdrawal of exemptions; superintendents of hospitals, asylums and staff of those institutions; teachers at schools for the deaf, dumb, and blind; one apothecary for each apothecary store; superintendents and operators in wool and cotton factories, paper mills, superintendents and managers of wool carding machines, with a provision as to profit similar to that applicable to other tradesmen; presidents and teachers of colleges, academies, schools, and theological seminaries who were engaged in those activities for two years prior to the passage of the act; workers in arms and other munitions, saddles, harnesses and army supplies which were necessary to such businesses; workers engaged under contracts with the government to furnish arms and other munitions, provided that persons employed by the states furnish the products to the states; those constructing ships and related articles of war; those engaged in the manufacture of salt up to twenty bushels a day, lead and iron, coke for the manufacture of iron, miners, and colliers; one male citizen for each five hundred head of cattle, each two hundred and fifty head of horses or mules, and five hundred head of sheep, provided no white male exempt from military duty was engaged in raising stock with that person; one person, or overseer, on each plantation on which a white person was required by ordinances or laws of any state and on which there was no white male not liable to service; one white male for every plantation with twenty Negroes or more, and one for every twenty Negroes on two or more plantations within five miles of each other, each having less than twenty Negroes; and such other persons as the President should feel ought to be exempted.[119] The exemption act of April 21 was repealed.[120]

As time passed, others were brought under the exemption laws. Contractors for carrying mail and drivers of post coaches and hacks

[119] *Confederate Laws*, 1 Cong., 2 Sess., 1862, c. XLV, [s. 1].
[120] *Ibid.*, c. XLV, s. 2.

were exempted in April, 1863.[121] To be exempted, the drivers had to use coaches or hacks because of the weight of the mail.[122]

Dissatisfaction was expressed with the changed law, particularly with regard to the provision concerning overseers. The North Carolina General Assembly resolved, on December 17, 1862, to instruct the North Carolina representatives in Congress to urge a repeal of this provision, as the members felt it meant unjust discrimination between those owning livestock or Negroes and those less fortunate. The Assembly added that the Bill of Rights, which declared that no man was entitled to privileges or emoluments except for public service, was violated.[123] On May 1, 1863, Congress repealed that portion of the act which exempted a person as overseer or additional police for every twenty Negroes.[124] There was a provision, however, for one person to be exempted on each plantation which was the sole property of a minor, an incompetent person, a *feme sole*, or a person away on military duty where there were twenty or more slaves, with the proviso that the exempted person must have been employed as an overseer prior to April 16 and that no adult white male, not subject to military duty, was on the farm or plantation. Owners of slaves were required to pay five hundred dollars for each person so exempted.[125] The President was authorized to exempt others to prevent a lack of white or slave labor necessary for the production of grain or other provisions for the support of the home population.[126]

In May, 1863, the Congress also extended the exemption to all state officers claimed by the governor of a state as necessary for the administration of government. This exemption was not to continue following the adjournment of the next regular session of a state legislature unless the state's lawmakers should exempt those persons from military duty in the Confederate Army.[127]

Despite the fact that vast numbers were exempted, still others felt unnecessarily excluded from the legal provisions which would protect them from military service. One W. H. Lineberry, a hatter, wrote to Jonathan Worth, "I have concluded to drop you a few lines altho I don't know that it hardly worth while to waist ink and paper on the subject which I am going to write about." He explained that nearly all "mechanicks" except hatters were exempted, told of his business, and stressed the need of the people for hats. Commenting on the desire for hats on the part of volunteers returning home, he said, "I

---

[121] *Ibid.*, c. XX, [s. 1].

[122] *Ibid.*, c. XX, s. 2.

[123] *Resolutions of a Public Nature, Passed by the General Assembly of North-Carolina, 1862-'63*, pp. 49-50. (Hereinafter cited *North Carolina Resolutions*.)

[124] *Confederate Laws*, 1 Cong., 3 Sess., 1863, c. LXXX, [s. 1].

[125] *Ibid.*, c. LXXX, s. 2.

[126] *Ibid.*, c. LXXX, s. 3.

[127] *Ibid.*, c. LXXX, s. 4.

Herd one say that he had rather go Barefooted than Bare Headed."
Lineberry, understanding that the President and Secretary of War were
empowered to exempt additional persons, suggested that the North
Carolina General Assembly pass a resolution in favor of hatters and
call their plight to the attention of the President.[128]

After the fall Congressional legislation, the newspapers were again
vocal. As the *Standard* commented, after printing the exemption bill,
"It could hardly be expected to meet with universal approval." The
paper was "gratified to learn that President Davis will exercise the
utmost forbearance in carrying into execution the last conscript law,
being aware how disastrously it must operate upon the poor farmers
especially, in those sections where there were few slaves. We are assured that he will not call out the conscripts under the last act until
the necessity becomes imperative." The paper reported that North
Carolina had done about four times as much as other Southern states
under the first conscript law, and it suggested that the legislature demand full compliance from all states under the first law before putting
the new enactment into effect.[129] A few days later, a special order dealing with the enrollment of men between eighteen and forty was published.
Again, the newspaper emphasized the need for full compliance from all
states, pointing out that North Carolina had poured "blood and treasure
. . . out for the defence of the South, although her own territory has
been shamefully neglected. In high places at Richmond, it is admitted
that she has done more than her duty." The article continued by
questioning the justness of taking more of the state's population for the
defense of Virginia before other states filled their quotas under the first
conscription law.[130]

The Raleigh *Register*, too, discussed conscription. Saying that it
did not doubt the constitutionality of the law and the necessity for it,
the paper commented that "the mode recently adopted for executing it
in this city is unnecessarily harsh, and well calculated to bring odium on
a law so necessary to our success in this war." The report explained
that men were picked up at the point of a bayonet if they could not
produce certificates of exemption immediately, and embarrassment to
two citizens was cited as proof of the lack of tact employed by officers.[131]

Military personnel proceeded to carry out the new conscription law.
General orders issued from the Adjutant General's office on November
27, 1862, instructed commanding officers of the militia to call out their
regiments and enroll men between eighteen and forty who were liable
for military duty. The orders outlined dangers facing the state, urging

[128] W. H. Lineberry to Jonathan Worth, December 11, 1862, in Hamilton,
Worth Papers, I, 213-215.
[129] Raleigh *Standard*, October 15, 1862.
[130] *Ibid.*, October 29, 1862.
[131] Raleigh *Register* (Semi-Weekly), December 6, 1862.

officers "to use all diligence in arresting deserters and absentees without leave from the army. . . . The brave and patriotic soldier will not over stay his furlough unless providentially hindered. The coward alone will shirk (at home) whilst his braver comrades endure the heat and burthen of the fight."[132]   Difficulties in enforcement continued to plague the military authorities, and early 1863 was a critical period. The situation was so bad in Yadkin County, where twenty to thirty conscripts lodged themselves in a schoolhouse and fought the militia, that the situation in the mountain section was soon out of the control of the military forces.[133]

Though enforcement of the law proceeded, there was concern with regard to conscription, and both private and official correspondence indicated the same feeling of worry. Even Jefferson Davis, in a letter to Governor Vance, admitted that "The Conscript Act has not been popular any where out of the Army." He explained that those in the army felt that the burden was being distributed equitably by virtue of the law.[134]   Referring to a request from Vance concerning exemption by executive action of those caring for lunatics and idiots, Davis said he could not accept the suggestion, that he interpreted the section of the law relative to executive action to be applicable to individual cases and not classes, "and in the present reduced condition of so many regiments it is necessary that the law should be rigidly construed."[135]   On the other hand, extenuating circumstances were at times considered. Vance later wrote to endorse a request from senators and representatives of the tenth Congressional District that the law be suspended in that district because of the difficulty of getting labor, the suffering of families, and other hardships. Several endorsements were on the letter. One, initialed "J. D.," indicated that it was proper to grant relief "by enrolling and leaving at home for the present the men of this district as a reserve, subject to future call."[136]

Individuals also sought information and advice relative to the operation of the law. Two soldiers, stationed in Virginia, wrote to Jonathan Worth, explaining that they were "twelve months vollin tears in the surves of our State" and were over thirty-five years of age. They said the twelve-month period was up and they did not want to re-enlist, though they were willing to be detailed to some government work. They promised to pay "etch of us" fifty dollars if Worth would get

[132] *Ibid.*, December 13, 1862.
[133] Barrett, *The Civil War in N.C.*, pp. 185-186.
[134] Jefferson Davis to Zebulon B. Vance, November 1, 1862, in Johnston, *Vance Papers*, I, 296.
[135] Davis to Vance, November 29, 1862, in *Official Records*, Series IV, I, 218.
[136] Vance to Davis, December 19, 1863, and endorsements thereon, in *Official Records*, Series IV, I, 246-248.

such work for them.[137]   Another individual, J. W. Ellis, applied to the Secretary of War for a discharge on the ground of his official responsibilities as a North Carolina legislator.   The Secretary explained that neither the law of October, nor that of April, worked to discharge a person from service, though furloughs had been extended to members of the North Carolina legislature for a period to extend one week beyond the expiration of the session.[138]

The beginning of 1863 saw the same problems, though perhaps intensified, as had existed throughout the months of 1862.   A circular issued in January by the Adjutant and Inspector General's Office in Richmond called attention to the great necessity for "strenuous exertions" in securing soldiers.   Officers were to be detailed for the duty of "gathering Conscripts," and the officers were to offer encouragement, "consistent with the law and the regulations of the service, and by kind treatment and arguments addressed to the patriotism and sense of duty of citizens, to induce them to enter the service of their country."   Conscripts were to be permitted to join any company and regiment needing recruits within the command of the recruiting officers.   Those conscripts who offered themselves were to be given the privileges of volunteers. Officers engaged in this activity were also called on to "apprehend all stragglers from the Army in their reach."[139]   The intent of the circular was evidently misinterpreted, for General Orders No. 16, issued a month later, indicated that the January paper was not to supersede the conscription law.   The orders revealed that reports had been received which showed that some officers were virtually setting aside the system. Officers were, therefore, ordered to refrain from interfering with conscripts already in the custody of other officers, to respect certificates of exemption, and to grant no such certificates themselves.[140]   As late as April, a letter to Peter Mallett revealed that the interference referred to in the order was still a problem.[141]

Desertions also plagued the military authorities, and men assigned to the duty of arresting deserters generally doubled their work and sought conscripts at the same time.   For example, Marmaduke S.

[137] John Presnell and William W. Nelson to Jonathan Worth, December 11, 1862, in Hamilton, *Worth Papers*, I, 212.
[138] James A. Seddon to J. W. Ellis, December 8, 1862, in *Official Records*, Series IV, II, 231.
[139] Circular, January 8, 1863, filed with records of *In re* Samuel H. Johnson, in Original Records of the North Carolina Supreme Court, 1863, Office of Clerk of the Supreme Court, Raleigh.   (Hereinafter cited as Original Supreme Court Papers.)
[140] General Orders No. 16, February 7, 1863, filed with record of *In re* Samuel H. Johnson, Original Supreme Court Papers, 1863.
[141] G. L. Lay to Peter Mallett, April 13, 1863, filed with record of *In re* Samuel H. Johnson, Original Supreme Court Papers, 1863.

Robins was ordered to detail three men from his company, between the ages of forty and forty-five to help arrest conscripts and deserters.[142]

Not only did military and governmental officers have to wrestle with problems of desertion and conscription, but the matter of exemptions created supplemental worries and difficulties which had to be faced by these men.   President Davis and Governor Vance corresponded at length on the subject of exemptions for state employees, with Vance referring to the "extreme rigor" with which the conscript law had been enforced in North Carolina.   He mentioned a letter indicating that officers or agents necessary to the administration of state government would be exempted. After referring to the exemption bill of October 11, 1862, Vance stated that the state government was authorized by law to determine necessity and that executive and judicial officers were to be exempted except for militia duty requirements.   The Governor concluded that any other construction of the law would result in the abolition of state government.[143]   Vance, writing to the Bureau of Conscription the same day, referred to the strict adherence to the law followed by his state; he expressed again the opinion that conscription of the state's officers would result in a cessation of government.   He stressed the fact that North Carolina law provided that none should be exempted from militia duty should invasion or insurrection occur.[144] This question of the responsibility and liability of state officers was also the subject of Supreme Court review, a question to be discussed later.

Exemptions were granted regularly.   A record of thirty-one men examined at Camp Holmes on April 1 and 2, 1863, showed that five of the number were exempt and three were exempted for specified periods of time, ranging from three to twelve months.[145]

Various claims for exemption were made, and numerous instructions were given.   A circular from the Bureau of Conscription in Richmond, issued March 30, 1863, explained that claims for exemption and details because of work with contractors with the government would not be considered unless the specified procedure was followed.   Applications were to be made through officers with whom contracts were made or upon their recommendations for certificates.[146]   The North Carolina Conscript Office notified prospective conscripts, on April 8, 1863, that the camp of instruction was the only place at which substi-

[142] William F. Foushee to Marmaduke S. Robins, February 23, 1863, in Robins Papers.
[143] Zebulon B. Vance to Jefferson Davis, March 31, 1863, in *Official Records*, Series IV, II, 464-465.
[144] Zebulon B. Vance to G. J. Rains, March 31, 1863, in *Official Records*, Series IV, II, 465-466.
[145] Record of Recruits Examined at Camp Holmes, April 2, 1863, in Mallett Papers.
[146] Raleigh *Register* (Weekly), April 15, 1863.

tutes could be received. No enrolled conscript had the right to place a substitute in any company in service, but he had to offer his replacement at a camp of instruction.[147]

Because of these and other requirements, individuals encountered difficulties in their endeavors to obtain exemption. D. G. Worth wrote to Jonathan Worth of his troubles resulting from his lack of knowledge as to the specific age of his substitute. The enrolling officer required such information, and Worth knew neither where to find the boy nor his parents. He explained that he had finally obtained the father's address, written to the man about his plight, and asked the father to go before a magistrate and make an affidavit. On the basis of facts given in the paper taken to Worth by the father, an extension of four months was added to his original exemption period.[148] Another father swore in an affidavit that he was the father of one Pleasant Bodenhamer, deceased; that in February, 1862, the son had entered the army as a substitute for J. R. Welborn; that the boy had died May 1, 1862, "being not yet Eighteen Years of Age. . . ."[149]

A number of affidavits were filed for members of the Society of Friends, attesting to membership. In quite a few of these, the assistant clerk of the Meeting indicated that the particular subject of the affidavit was not a member of the Society on October 11, 1862, but was a member in good standing in September, 1863, and that the member professed "to be conscienciously [sic] bound against bearing arms," was believed to be sincere and was, therefore, recommended to the authorities for favorable consideration. Such petitions on behalf of those who had joined the Society after the date of the exemption bill were generally to no avail.[150]

Steps were also taken on behalf of students and teachers. David L. Swain, President of the University of North Carolina, wrote a long letter to Jefferson Davis in October, 1863, in which he included statistics on the number of students and faculty members who had gone into service. He suggested that "A rigid enforcement of the Conscription Act may take from us 9 or 10 young men with physical constitutions in general better suited to the great pursuits of literature and science, than military service." Swain predicted that the University would ultimately have to close its doors if too many withdrawals occurred. He pointed out the fact that faculty members were exempted,

[147] Salisbury *Carolina Watchman*, April 20, 1863.

[148] D. G. Worth to Jonathan Worth, January 24, 1863, in Hamilton, *Worth Papers*, I, 226-227.

[149] Affidavit of David Bodenhamer, August 24, 1863, in Guilford County Miscellaneous Papers, Archives, State Department of Archives and History, Raleigh. (Hereinafter cited Guilford County Papers.)

[150] See affidavits of Gideon Cox on behalf of John M. Fesmire, Joseph Allen, Harmon Cox, David Wrightman, Reuben T. Cox, James Fesmire, Orlendo E. Gardner, Joel F. Trogden, September 21 and 25, 1863, in Robins Papers.

and concluded that such action on the part of Congress implied that there was no intention to close institutions of higher learning.[151] Though the University managed to remain open through the War, other colleges were forced to close their doors,[152] and many students were conscripted.[153]

Many could sympathize with the viewpoint of one Freeman Hurdle, who wrote to his Uncle John in the summer of 1863:

> Uncle John you rote that you hadente gon in to the armey yete bute you expected that you woode have to goo soone. I donte blame you fore staying oute as longe as you cood fore if you knode as mutch a boute the wore as I doo you wode staye at home as longe as you coode.[154]

With the number of exemptions sought and granted, the job of filling quotas was increasingly difficult. Governor Vance indicated in July, 1863, that there were not enough men in the state to raise the seven thousand required "without resorting to the classes exempted from conscription as State officers, men with substitutes, &c., who would be entitled to discharge if made Confederate troops." He suggested that Davis recognize men remaining under Vance's control as state troops, which would include exempts, in satisfying the quota.[155] Davis replied that he would receive as many as would organize under the act for local defense and would accept militia or state troops for the remainder.[156]

President Davis had recommended in January, 1863, that there be revision in the exemption laws, saying that serious complaints regarding the inequality of the operation of the law had been received.[157] Congress adjourned in May without making changes.[158] The Raleigh *Register* consequently expressed the opinion that "Its mental calibre was not such as was expected from a constituency so intellectual as that of the Southern Confederacy." The paper felt it grossly unfair that no

---

[151] David L. Swain to Jefferson Davis, October 15, 1863, University of North Carolina Papers, Southern Historical Collection.

[152] Hugh Talmage Lefler and Albert Ray Newsome, *The History of a Southern State: North Carolina*. Revised Edition (Chapel Hill: The University of North Carolina Press, c. 1963), p. 498.

[153] Clarence D. Douglas, "Conscription and the Writ of Habeas Corpus in North Carolina During the Civil War," *Historical Papers* (Durham: Trinity College Historical Society, 1922), Series XIV, p. 15. (Hereinafter cited as Douglas, "Conscription.")

[154] Freeman Hurdle to his uncle (John F. Leach), July 31, 1863, filed with record of Freeman Hurdle v. John F. Leach, 63 N.C. 366 (1869), in Original Supreme Court Papers.

[155] Zebulon B. Vance to Jefferson Davis, July 2, 1863, in *Official Records*, Series IV, II, 617.

[156] Davis to Vance, July 2, 1863, in *Official Records*, Series IV, II, 617.

[157] Message of President Jefferson Davis, January 14, 1863, Confederate States of America *Senate Journal*, 1 Cong., 3 Sess. (1863), p. 15.

[158] See *Confederate Laws*, I Cong., 3 Sess., January 12-May 1, 1863.

steps had been taken to draft resident aliens, "living in our midst and enjoying the protection of our laws."[159]

Confusion reigned. To clarify the situation and to respond to many inquiries, the Bureau of Conscription issued another circular in the summer of 1863. It explained that the extension of the conscript age meant that substitutes under forty-five years of age and not otherwise exempt would not be acceptable. The circular further stated that in the future a person who furnished a substitute would become liable himself when the services of the substitute were lost for any reason other than casualty of war. Applications for exemption would be considered by local enrolling officers who would, in turn, refer them to higher authorities should there be doubt concerning the decision.[160]

Efforts to inspire men to join the army were made even after the conscription process was in force. An officer assigned the duty of visiting Virginia and adjacent states was told, "It is desired that you will on this mission employ every effort to reanimate our people, inspire them with hope and renewed zeal for the cause, and especially induce those liable to service to come forward to their places promptly, and without awaiting the regular process of conscription."[161]

The response to such efforts was less than enthusiastic, and by the end of 1863, the over-all situation was far from bright. General Robert E. Lee wrote that the armies in the field should be retained and recruited and that the law should be enforced impartially. He added, "The law should not be open to the charge of partiality, and I do not know how this can be accomplished without embracing the whole population capable of bearing arms, with the most limited exemptions. . . ." Lee shared the opinion that the exemption law was subject to much abuse, and that many escaped service who were only nominally within its provisions.[162] A report on conscription in North Carolina, South Carolina, Georgia, and Virginia indicated that for every three men in the army in those states, there were still two liable to conscription. Of those enrolled, about one-third were in the army, one-sixth detailed, and one-half exempted. The number of substitutes was estimated at five per cent, though the report showed that the percentage had been doubled by some estimates.[163]

The appointment of Colonel Thomas P. August, a Virginia native, as commandant of conscripts in North Carolina was unpopular. Though Governor Vance protested the appointment, August assumed the re-

[159] Raleigh *Register* (Weekly), May 6, 1863.

[160] *Ibid.*, July 29, 1863.

[161] Samuel Cooper to William Smith, August 13, 1863, in *Official Records*, Series I, XXIX, Part II, 645.

[162] Robert E. Lee to Jefferson Davis, November 29, 1863, in *Official Records*, Series I, XXIX, Part II, 853.

[163] T. P. August to S. W. Melton, November 7, 1863, in *Official Records*, Series IV, II, 939.

sponsibility.[164] Discussing the question of substitutes, Colonel August wrote that "There are a very large number of spurious substitute papers in the hands of persons who are remaining out of the Army until the validity of the papers can be passed upon. The number in all States, it is believed, will reach from 10,000 to 15,000."[165] A short time later, the Superintendent of the Bureau of Conscription wrote that there were then fifteen thousand cases of substitution under investigation.[166]

The Raleigh *Register* reported, on November 27, 1863, that North Carolina had furnished one hundred thousand men for the Confederate army. For the year ending July, 1863, the state had sent 11,874 conscripts and between three and four thousand volunteers. Included in the quota had been 2,040 substitutes. The paper listed other exempts: employees at the state asylum, 23; apothecaries, 18; blacksmiths, 588; county and state officers, 282; cadets at military institutes, 15; colliers, 11; Confederate States judicial officers, one; Confederate States tax collectors, two; details, 1,913; disabled persons, 7,868; persons exempted because of executive action, 87; express company employees, 14; foreigners, 117; factory employees, 155; fire department personnel, 57; foundry workers, six; government contractors, 28; hatters, three; harness makers, one; militia officers, 2,346; magistrates, 407; millers, 668; millwrights, 123; mail contractors and carriers, 73; miners, 36; non-combatants, 196; overseers, 120; operatives in iron works, 17; preachers, 156; physicians, 264; paper makers, 14; policemen, 34; printers, 54; postmasters and clerks, nine; railroad employees, 533; shoemakers, 651; salt makers, 627; school teachers, 121; state ordnance employees, 258; state agents, two; seamen, 11; steamboat agents, one; superintendents of gas works, two; tanners, 174; telegraph operators, 18; wagon makers, 29; wheelwrights, 13; powder manufacturers, three; government agents, 17; and others discharged on writs of habeas corpus, 31, making a total of 21,558.[167]

In January, 1864, a report on North Carolina, based on records in the Adjutant General's office, indicated that there were 80,957 men in the field; 4,602 exempted by reason of vocation; 25,000 exempted by claim of the Governor; 8,064 exempted by examining boards, or a total of 38,166 exempted. In all, 119,123 white males could be accounted for, but census figures showed that there were 132,000 white males between eighteen and forty-five. It was estimated that about a fourth of the unknown 12,877 had fled or were in portions of the country in which the law was inoperative, which left 9,658. The Adjutant General for

[164] Barrett, *The Civil War in N.C.*, p. 185.
[165] T. P. August to S. W. Melton, November 7, 1863, in *Official Records*, Series IV, II, 940.
[166] John S. Preston to James A. Seddon, December 31, 1863, in *Official Records*, Series IV, II, 1070.
[167] Raleigh *Register* (Weekly), November 27, 1863.

North Carolina had estimated that a number of early companies, made up of persons subject to conscription, were received into service when no adequate records were being kept. These, with those who joined old regiments to avoid conscription, were estimated to number 7,500. This meant there were still 2,158 subject to the law. The state had furnished 67,736 volunteers, 13,221 conscripts through camps, and 7,500 other conscripts—a total of 88,457. The report concluded that the disproportionate number of men in the field compared to the number exempted could be attributed to "requisitions made by the Governor of the State."[168]

During 1863, the North Carolina legislature was also concerned with the problem of exemptions from the militia. In February, the Governor was empowered to call out as militia all able-bodied men between eighteen and forty-five, but exempted were governmental officers, a salt commissioner for each county, specified numbers of blacksmiths and millers, ministers, officers and necessary staff members for the insane asylum and institute for the blind, deaf, and dumb and the inmates and pupils of those institutions, physicians who had practiced for four years prior to the passage of the act, various railroad officials and employees, an editor and necessary assistants for each newspaper, the president and teachers in colleges, the principal and teachers of academies, and a reasonable number of persons in the cotton, woolen, iron, leather and shoe industries who were working under Confederate or state contracts. The Governor was given power "in special and extraordinary cases to exempt any other person."[169]

A few months later an act concerning the militia and a guard for home defense contained a provision that exemptions from militia service would be granted for causes similar to those prescribed by Congress for exemptions from the conscription act.[170] The Governor was to enroll all white males not in service in the Confederate army between the ages of eighteen and fifty who were resident in the state, including foreigners who had been in North Carolina thirty days prior to enrollment, to serve as a home guard. High government officials, including the Governor, judges of the Supreme and Superior courts, members of the General Assembly, and others with comparable responsibilities were to be exempted. Again, too, the Governor was given authority to exempt other persons as he deemed it proper.[171] Members of the Society of Friends could be exempted upon payment of one hundred dollars, though prior payment of five hundred dollars under provisions of the Confederate laws would be accepted in lieu

---

[168] *Official Records*, Series IV, III, 98-99.
[169] *N.C. Public Laws*, Adjourned Session, 1863, c. 14, s. 1.
[170] *N.C. Public Laws*, Called Session, 1863, c. 10, s. 1.
[171] *Ibid.*, c. 10, s. 2.

thereof.[172] Additional exemptions were incorporated in the law in December, bringing the state law into conformity with that of the Confederacy.[173]

The Governor was given power to use members of the home guard to arrest conscripts and deserters in their own or adjoining counties;[174] authority to call out the militia for similar duty had been given in July.[175] Even before these enactments, however, commanding officers of the militia had been ordered to call out such portion of the regiments as were needed to arrest deserters. By order of Governor Vance, those who had furnished substitutes for the Confederacy were informed that they were not thereby exempted from militia duty under the provisions of the order of May 9, 1863.[176] The Governor also declined to exempt tanners, blacksmiths, and others in similar occupations from home defense duty.[177]

Considering the Confederate conscription acts, the state acts relative to the militia and the home guard, provisions with regard to exemptions from the Confederate army and from state duty, and orders from various military officers, it is obvious that legal questions would arise. The interpretation of these numerous laws and orders inevitably overlapped and conflicted. The result was reflected in the countless opinions handed down by Superior Court judges, by judges in chambers who rendered their individual opinions, and by the judges of the North Carolina Supreme Court sitting as a full Court. Interpretation of the legislation enacted in 1862 and in 1863 involved questions of constitutionality, jurisdiction, and procedure, as well as matters of individual rights and responsibilities. A study of these cases is vital to an understanding of the conscription and exemption laws as they were applied in North Carolina.

[172] *Ibid.*, c. 10, s. 5.
[173] *N.C. Public Laws*, Adjourned Session, 1863, c. 14, s. 1.
[174] *Ibid.*, c. 18, s. 2.
[175] See section 3 of act ratified July 7, 1863, following *Resolutions of a Private Nature Passed by the General Assembly of North Carolina, at its Adjourned Session of 1863*, and "accidentally omitted" from the published laws of the July, 1863, session.
[176] General Order No. 5, May 9, 1863, signed by Daniel G. Fowle, in Robins Papers.
[177] Order issued by Adjutant General's Office, August 31, 1863, in Robins Papers.

II

JUDICIAL INTERPRETATION OF 1862 AND 1863
LEGISLATION

The Confederacy was basically a weak government. Its very existence was dependent on the willingness of strongly independent states to give up cherished rights. Without relinquishing a certain degree of independence, the states were merely hastening the downfall of their hastily formed Confederate government. The clash between military and civil authorities was a plague to the successful operation of war. The lack of a court of last resort, on a federal level, was a weakness which was felt directly as the military and judicial officials determined questions of policy and regulation and interpretation and came up with differing answers. Though the Confederate Constitution, modeled closely after that of the United States, provided for a Supreme Court and inferior federal courts,[1] none was ever established and there was no higher court than the highest courts of the individual states of the Confederate States.[2]

Because of this lack of an appellate court in the federal system, the influence of state courts was of more than ordinary importance. The North Carolina Supreme Court during the years of the Civil War was presided over by three men—men whose decisions were of far-reaching magnitude, both as to the state and Confederate governments and as to individuals whose lives were thereby affected.

The Chief Justice, Richmond M. Pearson, was to voice the dissatisfaction of many North Carolinians with the policies of the Confederacy, and he faithfully adhered to his interpretation of the laws despite the fact that he was more often than not the representative of the dissenting point of view. His colleagues on the bench, Judges William H. Battle and Matthias E. Manly, both tended to uphold the validity of the Confederate laws and interpret them in a light favorable to the cause of the South.

The backgrounds of the three men were similar. All three were graduates of the University of North Carolina,[3] had served in the

[1] Henry Steele Commager, ed., "The Constitution of the Confederate States of America," *Documents of American History*. Third Edition (New York: F. S. Crofts and Co., 1944), pp. 382-383.

[2] Johnston, *Vance Papers*, I, lvi.

[3] Robert P. Dick, "Richmond M. Pearson," *Biographical History of North Carolina From Colonial Times to the Present*, 8 volumes. Edited by Samuel A. Ashe (Greensboro: Charles L. Van Noppen, 1906-1917), V, 296. (Hereinafter cited as Dick, "Richmond M. Pearson.") S. A. Ashe, "William Horn Battle,"

General Assembly,[4] and had had experience as Superior Court judges[5] before becoming members of the Supreme Court bench.

These three men heard cases individually, rendering decisions during the periods in which the Supreme Court was not sitting; they also heard cases as a formal body and handed down formal opinions. Some cases went before these judges initially, while others originated in hearings before Superior Court judges. Still other cases were taken to the state's highest Court on writs of certiorari, a procedure which enabled the entire Court to review a decision of an individual member of the Supreme Court rendered in chambers.

These decisions were to be the basis for controversy and misunderstanding between North Carolina's Governor Vance and the Confederate officials. North Carolina's citizens generally agreed that the Governor was right in his efforts to prevent the overruling of civil law by military force.[6]

The conflict between the military and the judicial officials was not confined to North Carolina and the South. The Union had similar legal problems, with no satisfactory legal precedents. Habeas corpus proceedings were employed to release drafted men in the North as they were in the South; conflicts also existed between state and federal authorities.[7]

By far the largest number of cases were brought in North Carolina by petitions for writs of habeas corpus, whereby a soldier attempted to obtain a decision resulting in his release from military service. The many such hearings in the state meant disruption to the military officials, commanded by the Court to appear with the petitioner at a specified time for a judicial review.

As early as the summer of 1861, a writ of habeas corpus was returned before Chief Justice Pearson. One Hamilton C. Graham and his guardian alleged in their joint petition that Graham had enlisted as a private in May, 1861, when he was twenty years of age, that he had taken the action without the consent of his guardian, and that he had an estate sufficient to support him without the necessity of enlistment. The petition alleged further that Graham was being detained against his will at an encampment near Raleigh. Consequently, Major Stephen D. Ramseur, the officer having Graham in his charge, was ordered to bring the boy to court. Ramseur's answer to the petition showed that

in *ibid.*, VI, 20. (Hereinafter cited as Ashe, "William H. Battle.") S. A. Ashe, "Matthias Evans Manly," in *ibid.*, VI, 359. (Hereinafter cited as Ashe, "Matthias E. Manly.")

[4] Dick, "Richmond M. Pearson," V, 300; Ashe, "William H. Battle," VI, 21; Ashe, "Matthias E. Manly," VI, 360.

[5] Dick, "Richmond M. Pearson," V, 298; Ashe, "William H. Battle," VI, 21; Ashe, "Matthias E. Manly," VI, 360.

[6] Johnston, *Vance Papers*, I, lv-lvii.

[7] Randall, *Constitutional Problems*, p. 252.

the boy had enlisted, had taken the oath, and had later been placed in the guardhouse for violation of orders. At the time of the hearing the petitioner was awaiting trial by court martial.

Judge Pearson, referring to the fact that he had consulted with Judges Battle and Manly, ruled that Graham was not entitled to discharge. Though the statute gave authority to raise ten thousand men by enlistment, the Judge reasoned that the word "men" was not restrictive and should be taken to mean "soldiers"; that it was invalid to argue that the enlistment was a contract which the petitioner was incapable of entering because of his age. Even if a voidable contract, the enlistment had established the relationship of officer and soldier. The Chief Justice concluded that Graham was guilty of disobedience, with the consequence of his unlawful act being lawful imprisonment. An attempt to avoid the consequences by impeaching the validity of the enlistment prior to a discharge under military law was futile. Any other conclusion would mean that "all order and discipline in the army would be subverted."[8]

The Graham case is not of particular importance, though it was cited as a precedent in later cases, but it was significant in that it was one of the first such cases to go to the Supreme Court. The interpretation of the 1862 conscription acts, in the light of the exemption laws passed in both spring and autumn months of the same year, resulted in numerous judicial decisions. A case of great importance—perhaps the "key" case among the many heard after the first conscription acts went into effect—was that involving one J. C. Bryan, in which the Court reviewed the entire matter of its jurisdiction over such questions as were therein presented. Bryan's petition for a writ of habeas corpus asserted that he was between the ages of eighteen and thirty-five, had procured a substitute who was received by Peter Mallett, major in command of the camp near Raleigh and chief enrolling officer for North Carolina; and had been granted a discharge by Mallett on July 29, 1862. Nearly a year later, on June 16, 1863, Bryan was arrested as a conscript under the second law for raising conscripts, that of September, 1862. At the time of the petition, Bryan was in the custody of Lt. J. D. H. Young, and he petitioned for a writ to inquire into the cause of his detention and for a discharge. Young, in his answer, admitted the facts to be substantially true and averred that he had arrested Bryan in consequence of an order issued by the enrolling officer for the Fifth Congressional District.[9]

Extensive arguments were presented on the question of the jurisdiction of the Supreme Court, the Superior courts, and individual judges in such cases. The fact that Governor Vance had informed judges that

---

[8] In the Matter of Hamilton C. Graham, 53 N.C. 416 (1861). Also see record filed in Original Supreme Court Papers.

[9] In the Matter of J. C. Bryan, 60 N.C. 1 (1863).

the Confederate Secretary of War objected to the release of citizens arrested as conscripts by officers after they had been discharged by the courts was revealed by Pearson. He said the Confederate officials contended that state courts had no jurisdiction over the subjects petitioning for writs of habeas corpus. Because of this attitude, Judge Pearson wrote to the President of the Confederate States, asking that he send the Attorney General to present the point of view of the Confederacy. The District Attorney was sent to represent the government and to argue that state courts had no jurisdiction in such cases. A long opinion was issued by the Court, holding "that it has jurisdiction and is bound to exercise it, and to discharge the citizen whenever it appears that he is unlawfully restrained of his liberty by an officer of the Confederate States."[10]

The question of unlawful detention necessarily involved the construction of the acts of Congress, and the key question was whether the Secretary of War and his subordinate officers or the judiciary would make the decisions. If the question was a matter for the judiciary, then the problem as to jurisdiction of state courts was relevant. The Court cited a Massachusetts decision of 1815, in which the North Carolina Supreme Court had concurred. That case had held that a soldier could be discharged on the ground that the enlistment was invalid if reviewed in the light of proper construction of a Congressional act. Also cited was an 1809 North Carolina case, in which a decision was given holding that the state court had jurisdiction to discharge a United States soldier.[11]

Cases heard by individual judges, though they had not been officially reported, were used as precedents. *In re* Mills, heard by Pearson the preceding winter, involved a man who had claimed exemption as a shoemaker. The Chief Justice said he had written to his colleagues, Battle and Manly, and they had assumed that the question of jurisdiction was settled. In all cases, Pearson had "set forth that the power of the State judges to put a construction upon the acts of Congress, so far as they involve the rights of the citizen (as distinguished from mere military regulations), is settled, and all of the other judges in this State who have issued writs of *habeas corpus* have so treated it...."[12] Though Confederate tribunals would have jurisdiction, and adjudication in those courts would settle the proper construction of legislation, the executive branch possessed no judicial power; and any powers of construction given to that branch of government by Congress would be subject to judicial review.[13]

The argument was advanced that Congress had vested in the Secre-

[10] *Ibid.*, at pp. 18-19.
[11] *Ibid.*
[12] *Ibid.*, at p. 20.
[13] *Ibid.*, at pp. 25-26.

tary of War and his officers quasi-judicial power by granting jurisdiction to hear questions involving conscription and to make decisions relative thereto. Procedure providing that a man could appeal from the enrolling officer to the commandant of conscripts, on to the Secretary of War, and then possibly on to the President was equivalent to vesting in the Secretary of War judicial powers. Feeling that those responsible for enforcement of the conscription acts would seek to increase the numbers in the army, Pearson said that such a procedure would result in construction of the statutes so as to include as many people as possible. The power to make rules and regulations did not give the Secretary judicial authority, and the idea that Congress intended to deprive citizens of all judicial remedy was unthinkable in Pearson's mind. Holding that the Court had jurisdiction to hear cases brought by writs of habeas corpus, the Chief Justice added that the Court "had no right to be influenced by considerations growing out of the condition of our country, but must act with a single eye to the due administration of the law, according to the proper construction of the acts of Congress."[14]

Judge Battle concurred. He showed that the states' reservation of powers included that part of state sovereignty necessary for the safeguard of the rights of individual citizens.[15]

Having determined the rights of state courts and of individual judges to issue writs of habeas corpus and to consider causes of detention under authority of the Confederate government, the Court then turned to the right of the Supreme Court itself to issue the writ and determine the case in open court. For several reasons, the Court held that it had this power. First, the common law gave jurisdiction in that every superior court of record had traditionally had power to issue the writ. Even had legislation denied this power, such denial would have been void, a conclusion confirmed repeatedly by the laws of both England and North Carolina. Second, even assuming the power had to be conferred by statute, that action had been taken by the act which established the Court. Judge Pearson referred to the many applications for writs of habeas corpus during the preceding few months. The investigation in this particular case, being more thorough than any prior thereto, was an affirmation of the Court's authority. The question of jurisdiction of a state court in cases in which arrest was justified under provisions of a Confederate statute, being moot to the Bryan case, was left open for consideration at another time.[16]

The questions of jurisdiction and power having been settled, the Court proceeded to hear arguments on the merits of the case. Citing the Irvin and Meroney cases as precedents, the Court held that Bryan

[14] *Ibid.*, at pp. 26-28.
[15] *Ibid.*, at pp. 28-34.
[16] *Ibid.*, at pp. 43-59.

was entitled to exemption and discharge.[17]   A full understanding of the Bryan case is dependent on a study of these two decisions.

In the Irvin case, the petitioner had been discharged after applying for a writ of habeas corpus on the ground that he had offered a substitute in July, 1862. The substitute, thirty-six years old and fit for military duty, had been accepted by Peter Mallett, and Irvin had been discharged from his liability under the act of April, 1862. The law was changed the following September, and the military authorities then took the position that the September enactment made all white males between thirty-five and forty-five years of age subject to military duty, including Irvin's substitute, Gephart. Being liable as a conscript himself, Gephart could no longer serve for Irvin, thereby invalidating Irvin's discharge. So argued the military authorities, but Judge Pearson heard the case in chambers at Richmond Hill and decided, on July 9, 1863, that Irvin should be discharged. He reasoned that the act of September did not embrace those men already bound to serve during the war as substitutes, that the power of the President to call into service those between thirty-five and forty-five did not include men already in the armed forces. Giving as an example the case of a boy under eighteen who had been accepted as a substitute, Pearson stressed the fact that the authorities well knew the boy would reach conscript age at the time he was accepted for service in lieu of his principal.[18] The question of Congressional power to enact legislation specifically making liable those who had earlier furnished substitutes was not then before the Court, and the Judge commented that the question was "one which, I trust, public necessity never will cause to be presented, as it would violate natural justice and shock the moral sense."[19]

The Meroney decision was held to come within the interpretation in the Irvin case. Despite the decision, military personnel arrested Meroney, saying that the Secretary of War did not consider the construction of the act of September " 'a sound exposition of the act.' "[20] Again, the Court questioned the power of the Secretary to act as a judge. The North Carolina Supreme Court held that the Secretary of War could construe acts of Congress, but his interpretation was subject to judicial review. Judge Pearson referred to section eight of

[17] *Ibid.*, at pp. 59-66.

[18] *In re* Irvin, 60 N.C. 60 (1863). See also *In re* Prince, 60 N.C. 195 (1863), in which the Court interpreted the fact that a certificate of exemption provided that the principal would be exempted until the substitute reached the age of eighteen to be mere surplusage. Where the substitute was under eighteen when he was accepted on March 5, 1862, before the passage of the conscription act of April, the factor of age was immaterial. The boy met the requirements of being able-bodied and fit for military service, and he was accepted as a substitute for the war. The principal was, therefore, discharged.

[19] *In re* Irvin, 60 N.C. 60 at 62 (1863).

[20] *In re* Meroney, 60 N.C. 64 (1863).

the act of April, 1862, providing that those not liable to duty could be received as substitutes for those subject to call. The section was interpreted to mean that persons fit for service, but not liable under the then existing law, could be received as substitutes under regulations prescribed by the Secretary of War. To say that such a person could be made liable by a succeeding law of Congress would be equivalent to the addition of another condition, and such could not be done. Therefore, Meroney was found to be entitled to exemption and discharge.[21]

As indicated above, the Court referred to both the Irvin and Meroney cases when considering the Bryan matter. Concurring with the Chief Justice, Judge Battle held that those persons between the ages of eighteen and thirty-five who had furnished substitutes did not come within the meaning of the act of September, 1862, as the September act provided a specific call for persons between the ages of thirty-five and forty-five. Volunteers and substitutes already in service were not subject to call; substitutes could not be taken from their principals by force of the act so as to subject the principal to call under the provisions of the April act. To render a principal liable, Judge Battle held that his discharge must have contained some express or implied condition. The Secretary of War had no authority to impose retroactive conditions which would result in liability on the part of the principal. Battle remarked that it was too late for the War Department to endeavor to remedy "the mischief by assuming to legislate under the name of regulations."[22]

The Confederate authorities were soon expressing consternation at the North Carolina decisions. An order from the Assistant Secretary of War to Mallett, on the subject of the Irvin case, stated that the act of April 16 provided that persons not liable to military duty could be received as substitutes under regulations of the Secretary of War; that under the provisions of General Order 64, of September 8, 1862, the Secretary provided that a principal would become liable to conscription when his substitute became subject to military duty unless he was exempted on some other grounds; that General Order 82, of November 3, 1862, had reiterated the same principle. These regulations meant that substitutes were accepted subject to the conditions as outlined. When the responsibility of the substitute for military duty arose under new legislation, he was no longer exempt and could no longer relieve the principal. The order to Mallett, issued May 11, 1863, concluded with the words, "The opinion of Mr. Ch. Justice Pearson is not regarded by the department as a sound exposition of the Act of Congress and you will not regard it in your official action as such."[23]

Subsequently, on May 24, Mallett wrote for instructions in light of

[21] *Ibid.*

[22] In the Matter of J. C. Bryan, 60 N.C. 1 at 59-66 (1863).

[23] J. A. Campbell to Peter Mallett, May 11, 1863, in Mallett Papers.

the Irvin decision. Reference was made to the War Department, and an endorsement indicated that a person released by a judge would stand on facts different from other cases falling within the same general principles, and that no arrest was to be made without a special report of the facts to the War Department so as to obtain specific instructions in the case. The War Department asked about Irvin's enrollment, the date he put the substitute into service, facts concerning the substitute, the date of Irvin's second enrollment, and for other pertinent information which had been presented to Judge Pearson.[24]

The conflict of opinion was the subject of newspaper discussion. An article, entitled "Conflict of Authorities," was carried in June, 1863:

> The *Register*, well pleased at the least pretext for assailing Gov. Vance, has a long, prosy, and very dull article, in which it attempts to show that Chief Justice Pearson has delivered an erroneous decision in the Irvin case, and that the Secretary of War has the right to say what is civil law in North Carolina. The eminent jurist of the *Register* . . . ought not to hide his light under a bushel, or flash it on the public at so late a period as to do no good. If he had laid down the law in advance, it might have been of some advantage to the Chief Justice and the Governor. It is hardly excusable in him to have withheld it so long, leaving them to decide and act upon the case in the dark. His decision comes too late.

> The Richmond *Enquirer* copies an article from a paper in this State, which in the profundity of its wisdom and legal knowledge declares, that because Governor Vance is *sustaining* the judiciary of the State he has combined in himself executive and judicial functions. This assumption contradicts itself. It is his sworn duty, as Governor, to see that the decisions of our Courts are enforced. Does that make him a judicial officer? Does that place him in the attitude of usurping judicial functions? What nonsense![25]

The paper continued by saying that the Governor had stated that no citizen who had been discharged on a writ of habeas corpus would be arrested a second time by the Secretary of War. The editor commented on his appeal to Congress to establish a supreme court, a step which had not been taken. Without such a court of last resort, the paper felt, the executive department had no right to interpret the law so as to bind state judges because neither the President nor the Secretary of War could act judicially.[26]

The courts continued to discharge the large majority of those who applied for writs of habeas corpus, despite the opposition from the military authorities. By the spring of 1863, the trend was becoming

[24] G. W. Lay, by order of J. A. Campbell, to Peter Mallett, May 30, 1863, in Mallett Papers.
[25] Salisbury *Carolina Watchman*, June 8, 1863, quoting the Raleigh *Standard*.
[26] *Ibid.*

evident. Judge Pearson's disposition to look with favor on petitions for discharge compelled Daniel G. Fowle, at that time Major General in the Adjutant General's Department,[27] to write to Pearson:

I also enclose for your consideration two or three extracts taken from letters forwarded to-day, to this office. These letters are constantly being forwarded from the different regiments. In many of these your name is mentioned, as the friend and protector of deserters and conscripts. The impression has gone abroad in the army that you intend to discharge every man brought before you under a H. Corpus. And the feeling is becoming very strong that no one Judge should have the power of nullifying an Act of Congress.

It is also objected that these decisions are made, affecting a law upon which our very salvation as a people depends, without giving the Confederate Authorities notice, so that their case may be properly presented. I am aware of the injustice done you, and have denounced the men who are circulating these slanders to your prejudice, but if it is consistent with your duty, I should like to be heard upon the legality of any order issued from this office.

You may rest assured Judge that the construction put upon your decision, is greatly injuring the Army. Last winter when the Legislature passed the Act, to authorise the Gov. to order out the Militia, I do not believe there was a man in the Legislature who doubted but that he had the power to order the Militia to arrest deserters. I have tried my best to see how the Gov. can order out the Militia to suppress "insurrection" and yet not have the power to order them out to enforce the laws passed by Congress— but as they are both contained in the same clause of the Constitution, I cannot perceive the distinction. The public safety may be endangered as much by Laws not being enforced as by "insurrection."

I have written this Judge, because I thought you ought to know the effect of these decisions. I can say, that every decision I have . . . [found] very conclusive, so far as the case was stated. I think that the order of May 15th destroys the force of your decision in Irwin's case, but you did not have that before you. I have not seen your decision about Militia officers or rather your reasons for it.

In case of any conflict between the Judiciary and the Executive Departments, I need hardly say, that I would resign my office, before coming into conflict with you. I have for you a son's affection. You had a child once who loved you more than I do, but none of your living children entertains for you more affection.[28]

[27] Beth G. Crabtree, *North Carolina Governors, 1585-1958: Brief Sketches* (Raleigh: State Department of Archives and History, 1958), p. 107.

[28] Daniel G. Fowle to Richmond M. Pearson, May 22, 1863, in Richmond M. Pearson Papers, Southern Historical Collection, University of North Carolina. (Hereinafter cited as Pearson Papers.)

Judge Pearson obeyed his conscience and throughout the months of the Civil War interpreted the law as he felt right. Case after case went before him. The military authorities advanced technical arguments in many instances, as they did in the case of Elias Ritter. This man, when North Carolina was called on for troops early in 1862, had been summoned for service. He hired one Medlin to go as his substitute for three years or the war. Medlin was received; Ritter was discharged. This action occurred before passage of the April act; and that act did not encompass the petitioner, who was over the age limits set forth at that time. The September act, however, included those in Ritter's age group, as he was under forty-five; and he was called again and was held against his will. The officers argued that no company had been organized at the time the substitute went into the army. Ritter could not have, therefore, complied with War Department regulations of October 20, 1861, which had provided that a non-commissioned officer or soldier of the voluntary service who wished to furnish a substitute should obtain written consent from the captain of his company and from the commander of the regiment or corps. The regulations also required that the substitute obtain a certificate of fitness for service and show that he had been mustered into service for the war. The substitute would then be permitted to join the regiment or corps of the principal, who would, in turn, be entitled to discharge and an exemption certificate. Judge Pearson, after hearing arguments in the case, decided that the October circular was also applicable to companies in the process of formation. In such cases, a substitute could be received without the formality of carrying out the details required when one was replacing a man already in service. The object of acquiring able-bodied men for military duty was fulfilled when the substitute stepped in to take the place of another man when a company was being formed. Ritter was discharged.[29]

Even where there was suspicion of fraud a man was discharged. In February, 1863, one Boyden volunteered in a cavalry company, but on March 1, he procured a man named McLendon to take his place and enter an infantry company as his substitute. A certificate of exemption was obtained from the militia on the ground that a substitute had been employed. Another certificate showed that Boyden furnished McLendon as his substitute in a foot company and a horse for the cavalry. McLendon, who was fifty-one years old, was paid fifty dollars. In August, 1863, Col. Mallett was notified that fraud had been practiced on an "old man" and on the government by Boyden. An affidavit was introduced to show that McLendon had enlisted as a volunteer rather than as a substitute. On suspicion that Boyden had not engaged McLendon before he took the oath, Boyden was arrested. Much testimony

[29] In the Matter of Elias Ritter, 60 N.C. 76 (1863).

was introduced. It was shown that Boyden heard that McLendon was willing to go as a substitute for fifty dollars but that he was not a good rider and could not, therefore, join the cavalry. McLendon was heard to say he was going as Boyden's substitute when he inquired about county support for his wife and children. He went into service with the belief that his family would be provided for, but on learning that this information was not true, he asked Boyden to release him; Boyden refused. There was conflicting testimony as to the time of the agreement between Boyden and McLendon.

Judge Pearson, hearing the case at Richmond Hill, in the fall of 1863, decided that the case did not fall within the provisions of the Ritter case since Boyden was not drafted. Regulations permitting the transfer of a man from one company to another were cited. Pearson reasoned that the facts that neither company was organized and attached to a regiment and that one was infantry and the other cavalry were immaterial. Papers of exemption had been cleared several times, so the only question involved was that of fraud. Because he felt that the question of fraud was inconclusive, the Chief Justice discharged Boyden.[30]

Repeatedly the North Carolina Supreme Court held that petitioners were entitled to discharge because they had furnished substitutes and the facts were sufficient to bring the cases within one or more of the leading decisions, particularly those of Bryan, Irvin, and Ritter.[31]

There were situations in which the petitioners lost in their legal battle to obtain a discharge from the army. The well-known adage, "Ignorance of the law is no excuse," was applied to James M. Duke when he applied for a writ of habeas corpus on the ground that he had

[30] *In re* Boyden, 60 N.C. 175 (1863).

[31] See, in the Original Supreme Court Papers, the records of the following petitioners who were discharged: Simon E. Hodges. Lenoir County, discharged in June, 1863; Joel Wells, Alamance County, discharged in 1863; Elias Garner, Moore County, discharged in June, 1863; Adam Garner, Moore County, discharged in June, 1863; John F. Garner, Moore County, discharged in June, 1863; Richard G. Ward, Onslow County, discharged in June, 1863. The following records are in Guilford County Papers: William Wyrick, discharged in December, 1863; Orlando Lamb, discharged in November, 1863; David N. Woodhouse, discharged in October, 1863; Christopher Fields, discharged in October, 1863; Joel R. Welborn, discharged in October, 1863; William M. Kinne, discharged in October, 1863; Thomas Jordan, discharged in October, 1863; David Jordan, discharged in October, 1863; Levi Houston, discharged in October 1863. The following record is in Chatham County Confederate Papers, Archives, State Department of Archives and History: William A. Abernathy, discharged in December, 1863. (Hereinafter cited as Chatham County Papers.) The record of Joel Matthis, discharged November 19, 1863, is in the Cumberland County Miscellaneous Court Records, Archives, State Department of Archives and History. (Hereinafter cited as Cumberland County Papers.) These are by no means all of the cases involving exemptions because of substitutes, but they do give an idea of the volume which went to the judges of both the Superior and Supreme courts.

furnished a substitute.   Judge Battle determined that the writ could not be granted because the petitioner failed to allege that the substitute had been received as a soldier for three years or the war.   The man was bound by the fact that he had actually served after being called a second time.   When the enrolling officer had informed Duke of his liability, he had entered the army, had served, and had received payment for his services.   The fact that the petitioner was ignorant provided no excuse, and he was remanded to the custody of the military authorities.[32]

Again a denial occurred when one Curtis, a minister of a Primitive Baptist Church, claimed exemption because of his occupation.   He had agreed to enter the army in October, 1862, as a substitute for one Foster in Virginia; and he had traveled seventy miles, as far as Salisbury, when he was arrested as a conscript.   He sued out a writ of habeas corpus.   Holding that Curtis had subjected himself to conscription when he gave up his regular ministerial duties and entered the agreement to go as a substitute, the Court refused to discharge him.   The explanation was given that exemptions were "not for the purpose of conferring a special privilege on individuals. . . ."   The implication of the law was that exemption status should cease to exist when services were no longer rendered to those at home by the person holding exempt classification.   The law was enacted with the view of maintaining an army in the field while providing for adequate support for those at home.   To release men who had abandoned their careers of service in order to go into service as substitutes would be contrary to the intent of the law, according to the reasoning of Chief Justice Pearson.   The Judge did not discuss the question of the validity of the substitute agreement, considering the liability of Curtis for military service, saying the point did not have to be determined in the case before him.   He assumed, however, that until articles of enlistment were signed the substitution would be valid.[33]

Many, many cases involved substitutes, but other provisions of the exemption acts also came within the scrutiny of the judiciary.   Some men tried first one avenue of escape and then another, proving their persistence if not their bravery.   One of the most determined draft dodgers sought exemption in several ways.   He alleged that he had furnished a substitute, that he was a miller, and that he was a deputy sheriff.[34]   Various affidavits in the record gave both sides of the questions involved in the case.   One affiant stated that he had known the petitioner for life, that he was not a miller, but that "he was for four or thereabout years engaged in selling whiskey & farming on a small

[32] *In re* James M. Duke, Wayne County, July, 1863, in Original Supreme Court Papers.

[33] *In re* Curtis, 60 N.C. 180 (1863).

[34] *In re* Samuel H. Johnson (also spelled Johnston), 1863, in Original Supreme Court Papers.

skale."[35] A letter from the chaplain of the 45 Regiment, North Carolina Militia, read:

It is the *Duty* of *Some person* to bring again to your Notice the Case of the *Notorious* Samuel H. Johnston. In accordance with your last orders he was arrested by the officers of the Company to which he belonged, in view of his being brot. to your Camp as a conscript. On his pledging his word and honor to report himself to your Camp on the day they (The Officers) were to take him down, They permitted him to leave Durham station by himself as they thought—to report himself to you one week after this he is back Never, as a Member of Capt. Camerons Artilery [*sic*] Company at Goldsboro on a furlough for five Days—Not having gone to your Camp. It now turns out that he has never yet Joined Camerons Company but is there . . . Gambling with the Men and Drinking with the officers. This is facts are from Two Sources—by Respectable Men who belong to the Company. Now Sir, If you wish Justice done to this Man you will detail a Squad, to arrest him in Goldsboro. . . . He is unquestionably the Greatest Case that has turned up during the War.[36]

Though the outcome of the case is not clear in the records, men were sent to arrest "the notorious Samuel H. Johnson" in the spring.[37] The next June, Johnson was seeking an escape on the grounds of being engaged in milling, and he also tried to show at one time that he was a law enforcement officer. A return to the writ issued by Judge Battle, at the time of the petition claiming exemption as a miller, indicated that Private Samuel H. Johnson was then enlisted as a member of the company of Capt. Henry Dixon of Lenoir County, and that the petitioner was detained in that company.[38] The case is cited, despite the uncertainty as to its final outcome, to show the difficulty which one individual could cause the authorities when he was determined to carry out his intention to avoid service as long as possible.

Exemptions granted to millers were rather commonplace. A leading case, that of a thirty-three year old miller named Nicholson, served as a precedent for other cases involving tradesmen. Nicholson had worked as a boy with his father as a millwright. He enrolled in Guilford County on July 8, 1862, under the provisions of the April law. The enrolling officer informed the men that they had the right to volunteer before July 15, but if they did not do so, they were to appear on that date with rations for three days and proceed to a camp of instruction near Raleigh. Nicholson applied for exemption as a miller and millwright between the eighth and fifteenth of July, and he returned to the

---

[35] Affidavit in record of Samuel H. Johnson, in Original Supreme Court Papers.

[36] John A. McMannus to T. P. August, March 24, 1863, in record of Samuel H. Johnson, in Original Supreme Court Papers.

[37] See notes on back of letter from McMannus to August, cited above.

[38] See numerous affidavits, letters, and other documents in record of Samuel H. Johnson, in Original Supreme Court Papers.

mill late in August.   Before returning, he applied for work at the armory of H. C. Lamb and Company, and his name was included by Lamb in a list of persons he asked to have detailed to him.   Nicholson began working for Lamb, but he left September 29, against the wishes of Lamb.   Though the matter was reported to the military authorities, Lamb later received a letter detailing men to him, including Nicholson. Early in October, Nicholson was arrested, but he was told by the colonel to return to work in the mill.   The next January, Nicholson confided to his brother that he feared arrest and thought he would leave the community.   He did go to Virginia, but he returned in February to see his wife for a few days.   On a second trip from Virginia, in March, he was arrested in Forsyth County.   He told the sergeant who arrested him that he had considered deserting to the Yankees but thought better of the idea when he considered the disgrace which would fall on his family.   He had passed himself in Virginia as an exempt millwright.[39]

The Supreme Court, in reviewing the case, was faced with the question involving the correct application of the exemption act of October 11, 1862.   Did it apply only to the conscription act of September or to both that of September and that of April?   Citing the cases of Mills, a shoemaker, and Angel, a wagonmaker, the Supreme Court, through Chief Justice Pearson, decided that the exemption act of October was applicable to both the spring and fall conscription acts. He reasoned that Congress, by repealing the April exemption act, intended to replace exemptions outlined in the first law with one over-all exemption act.   Any other interpretation would mean that governors, legislators, judges, and other high officials would be subject to conscription.   The argument advanced to counter such reasoning was that the President had power to make special exemptions, which would take care of such situations as those mentioned, but the Judge determined that Congress had no such intention.   Though he had to admit that a retroactive construction, which would be the natural result of applying the exemption act of October 11 to the conscription act of April, would present difficulties, the Chief Justice felt that the interpretation was unavoidable.

The opinion of Pearson also contained a discussion of "the time" required by law for a person to be employed at his trade; if "the time" in Nicholson's case was set as that time when he was ordered into service, he was entitled to exemption and his subsequent conduct would not be held against him because such conduct was induced by unauthorized action of the military officers.   If, on the other hand, "the time" was October, when the exemption act was passed, then Nicholson would be liable as a conscript and would have no rights because he could not take advantage of his own wrong.   The exemption act stressed the

[39] *In re* Nicholson, June, 1863, record in Guilford County Papers.

necessity of actual employment in a field or trade, but it did not refer to the time when the person claiming such exemption was to be actually employed at that trade. The conscription act of September made it clear that "the time" was that at which the party was called into service. Pearson concluded that "the time" so far as the April act was concerned also meant that time when the party was ordered into service.

After detailed discussion of the laws involved, Judge Pearson decided that Nicholson had received no pay and no bounty and that he had done nothing to waive his rights of exemption. The law exempted all shoemakers and other specified artisans, not excepting those who were in the army or should have been there, when the act was passed. Concluding that the October exemption act as it related to the April conscription act had to be given relation to the time a person was actually ordered into service and removed from his trade, Judge Pearson decided the case in Nicholson's favor. He also discussed the invalidity of the repeal of the April exemption act if there had been no intention to apply the additional exemptions granted in the October act to persons under thirty-five years of age. Nicholson was discharged, and the enrolling officer was charged the costs of court.[40]

The Nicholson and related cases were cited as precedents in numerous other cases in which millers asked for and received exemption and discharge.[41] Occasionally the facts warranted a negative decision, as they did when Peter Cobb alleged he had been inducted into the army on July 8, 1862, against his consent. In August he was sent to Virginia, but the following May he returned to his home in North Carolina on a sick furlough. While at home, he presented an affidavit to the effect that he was a miller, had a wife and four children, owned no slaves; and he further alleged that his wife's attempt to carry on the business had resulted in the mill being "attended to imperfectly. . . ." Though no reason was given for the decision denying the petition, the Court evidently concurred with the military authorities who showed that Cobb had been in the army for months before he petitioned for exemption.[42]

About as numerous as millers were the blacksmiths. The leading case was that of Solomon N. Guyer, a man who had worked at his trade for ten years. In May, 1862, he was employed by one B. Weathersbie, who was working for the state. Though enrolled as a conscript, Guyer was detailed to Weathersbie and stayed there until the termination of the contract in March, 1863. Then he went to work for one Coffin as a blacksmith, and Coffin directed him to report to the enrolling officer

[40] *In re* Nicholson, 60 N.C. 68 (1863).

[41] Examples of cases involving millers are those of James A. Cole, discharged October 14, 1863; M. M. Wrightsell, discharged October 29, 1863; Nathan H. Wright, discharged October 30, 1863; James Clapp, discharged December 23, 1863, in Guilford County Papers. See also the record of Duncan Morrison, discharged October 14, 1863, in Cumberland County Papers.

[42] *In re* Peter Cobb, 1863, in Guilford County Papers.

and apply for exemption. The application was refused, and Guyer was sent to the camp of instruction near Raleigh. Again, the Court held that the exemption act of October 11 was applicable to the April conscription law. The Court stated that no person was entitled to exemption as a shoemaker, tanner, or other tradesman who was in the army on the date the act was passed, but those not placed in service prior to the passage of that act would be entitled to discharge. The number of artisans being insufficient to supply the needs of the public, provision was made for those at home to continue at their trades as long as possible; those in military service in the field were not embraced by the act. Relying on the Nicholson case, and distinguishing the Guyer case in which the petitioner had received no bounty, pay, rations, or clothing up to the time of his arrival at camp with the facts in the matter of one Dixon, who was in the army as a conscript when the exemption bill was passed, who had received bounty, pay, and other emoluments of a soldier, the Court held that Guyer was entitled to a discharge.[43]

Relying largely on the Supreme Court decisions in the cases of Nicholson and Guyer, other groups of artisans were discharged, many of them by Superior Court judges. Judge Robert R. Heath heard a number of petitions of workers, and shoemakers,[44] wagonmakers,[45] and tanners[46] were discharged. Again, however, technicalities meant a contrary result to that desired by the petitioners in some appeals. For example, Barfield Grantham, a shoemaker, claimed exemption because of his occupation. The facts showed that he farmed, and that his shoemaking business was a sideline. Judge Battle's opinion held that the statute required that the trade be the regular occupation of a person, not an occasional one, and the discharge was denied.[47]

In April, 1863, contractors for carrying the mails and drivers of post hacks and coaches were exempted by Congressional action.[48] Resulting from this legislation were a number of discharges from those petitioning their right to exemption because of mail responsibilities.[49]

[43] In the Matter of Solomon N. Guyer, a Blacksmith, 60 N.C. 66 (1863).

[44] See, in Guilford County Papers, records of Stanford Woodyard, discharged October 28, 1863; Joseph H. Watt, discharged October 14, 1863; Madison Bowman, discharged October 26, 1863; Booten Bohannon, discharged October 27, 1863; Franklin H. Pickett, discharged October 14, 1863; William J. Hays, discharged October 14, 1863. In Davidson County Papers, see records of Jesse Shoaf, discharged in October, 1863, and Enos Lanning, discharged in October, 1863. In Cumberland County Papers, see record of John C. McLean, discharged November 17, 1863.

[45] See records of Lewis Smith, discharged October 27, 1863, and Hiram Coble, discharged October 27, 1863, in Guilford County Papers.

[46] See record of William G. Brown, Davie County, 1863, in Original Supreme Court Papers.

[47] In the Matter of Barfield Grantham, a Shoemaker, 60 N.C. 73 (1863).

[48] *Confederate Laws*, 1 Cong., 3 Sess., 1863, c. XX.

[49] See *In re* D. L. Bringle, June, 1863, and *In re* M. A. Bringle, June, 1863, in Original Supreme Court Papers.

After the passage of this law, the Post Office Department advertised for bids for carrying the mail, calling attention to the exemption status of mail contractors and drivers of mail stages.[50]

One of the most controversial provisions in the exemption act was that involving overseers. Despite public disapproval in some areas, the North Carolina Supreme Court upheld the right of this group to exemption when the requirements of the law were fulfilled. Henry C. Huie, a man twenty-nine years old who lived in Cabarrus County, petitioned for exemption, saying his mother and a young daughter were the only white people on the neighboring plantation, and that he and his family lived on the adjoining place. He managed his own thirteen or fourteen Negroes and served as overseer for his mother. Huie was afflicted with bronchitis and was not, therefore, enrolled when other conscripts left the county. He had, however, reported on October 11, 1862, at the camp of instruction near Raleigh. The examining physician had found him incompetent to perform the duties of a soldier because of his health, and he was excused until May 1, 1863. His name was added to the roll in October, 1862, but he returned to his home and remained there until he was arrested.

In considering Huie's situation, Judge Pearson again ruled that the exemption act of October, and the May amendments thereto, were applicable to both the April and the September conscription acts. Col. Mallett insisted that the petitioner was enrolled on October 11, 1862, and that he had been in service since that date and was not, therefore, an overseer. Pearson determined that the mere fact that a man's name was put on a list did not mean that he was put in actual or constructive service, because the doctor had found his unfit at that time. Replying to that argument, the military officials said that the Secretary of War, through the Adjutant General, had held that persons unfit for service could be enrolled and used in hospitals or comparable institutions. The authority of the Secretary to use for other types of service conscripts unfit for military service in the field was questioned and a negative decision reached. The Chief Justice, as he had done so many times before, stressed the fact that the executive branch of the government did not possess judicial power. Concluding that the so-called enrollment of October 11 was void and that the petitioner was an overseer at the time of his arrest, on October 11, on April 16, and for several years prior thereto, the Court found Huie entitled to exemption.[51] Many other cases involving overseers were to be heard in 1864, after changes were made in the law in February of that year. The overseer provisions of the exemption laws were perhaps the most hated, the feeling being strong that the rich were favored by this provision while the poor received no benefits.

[50] Raleigh *Register* (Weekly), April 22, 1863.
[51] *In re* Huie, 60 N.C. 165 (1863).

Professional people, too, used the courts in their eagerness to remain outside the army. A surgeon dentist, who had practiced since 1856, petitioned for discharge because of his status as a physician. After reviewing evidence concerning instruction required in dental colleges, Judge Pearson decided that a dentist was a specialist in the medical profession and was entitled to a discharge.[52] Another physician who claimed exemption had his petition disallowed because he had been working for the salt commissioner for three months. He had used slaves and teams for the work and felt that these facts should not prevent his being granted an exemption. Because of the negative decision made by the military authorities, the man petitioned for a writ of habeas corpus, which was granted by Judge Pearson on June 29, 1863. The outcome was unusual. The colonel refused to admit the sheriff within the lines of his regiment to serve the writ on the captain to whom the writ of habeas corps was addressed. The back of the petition merely contained a notation giving this information.[53] Considering other cases heard by Judge Pearson, it is likely that the man would have been discharged had the case been heard. When the success of the military authorities, by means of this simple maneuver, is realized, it is indeed a wonder that the same tactic was not used in other cases.

Not only doctors but teachers, too, sought exemption. Moore W. Dollahite claimed exemption under the provision of the law which excused presidents and teachers of colleges, academies, and similar institutions under specified conditions. He alleged that he had been a teacher for ten or twelve years; and though his school had been suspended for twelve or eighteen months because of the "troubled condition of the country," he was teaching elsewhere at the time of his enrollment. The Bureau of Conscription in Richmond had denied the exemption, a decision in which Judge Battle concurred. The Judge based his opinion on the ground that the Court might disagree with the Bureau as to the time at which status was fixed in some of the enumerated classes, but the act with regard to physicians and teachers was explicit. The law required teachers to have been employed in their profession for two years prior to the passage of the October 11 act. The petitioner was remanded to the custody of the military authorities.[54]

Still others sought civilian status because of either their age or their physical infirmities. One John S. Gainey introduced rather nebulous evidence when he sought to prove his claim of age by using a family

[52] In the Matter of Hunter, 60 N.C. 372 (1864). Though reported with cases decided at the June, 1864, term, the case was dated December 4, 1863, at Richmond Hill.

[53] *In re* G. L. Sellars, New Hanover County, 1863, in Original Supreme Court Papers.

[54] In the Matter of Moore W. Dollahite, a School Teacher, 60 N.C. 74 (1863).

Bible which recorded the births of others in the family but not his own. The answer to the petition showed that Gainey had responded to the public notice for all between eighteen and forty-five to enroll and had, at that time, reported his age as being under forty-five. Despite this, and with no reason given, he was discharged by Superior Court Judge James W. Osborne on October 8, 1863.[55]

A rather pathetic case involved Alvis Craver, a minor who had gone as a substitute for Jesse T. Eaton with the clear understanding that the boy would not have to leave Salisbury. There was an agreement to the effect that the principal would go himself or find another substitute if orders did come for the boy to leave that town. Poor Alvis was sent to Virginia, put in action, and soon returned home on sick leave. At that time he was just over sixteen years of age, so his father petitioned for release of the boy. Alvis was arrested for being away without leave, but Judge Pearson allowed the father's petition for custody and discharged the boy. Again, no reasons for the decision were given.[56]

The subject of physical unfitness was one on which even Chief Justice Pearson was strict. He explained that a proper construction of the law required a certificate of unfitness after examination by a surgeon or board of surgeons appointed for the purpose. Without such evidence, no discharge could be granted.[57] Some endeavored to prove unfitness by affidavits, as did B. G. Craven, a man who claimed to be deaf. His affiant told of the man's circumstances, saying he was the only man in his neighborhood to help wives of soldiers in getting wood and other necessities except for an "old man or so over sixty." The back of the affidavit contained a notation, signed by J. M. Settle, that the man claiming the handicap "thinks he was exempted, but if he was not I would suggest that he be not. From *undertone* conversations with the party I am forced to believe his deafness not excessive." The man was ordered to report.[58]

Probably the most trying cases involved state officers. Because of the many government employees who claimed exemption, the problem became acute to Confederate authorities. Numbers of legal decisions were made in this area. A leading case involved F. W. Kirk, a man thirty-one years of age who claimed exemption because of his position as captain of the militia of Yadkin County. The return to the writ of habeas corpus indicated that Kirk had been taken into custody pursuant to verbal orders of Governor Vance to arrest militia officers of Yadkin and Wilkes counties as persons subject to conscription. The act of

[55] *In re* John S. Gainey, 1863, in Cumberland County Papers.
[56] *In re* Jacob Craver, 1863, in Original Supreme Court Papers.
[57] In the Matter of J. C. Bryan, 60 N.C. 1 at 24 (1863).
[58] Affidavit of Henry M. Foust, n.d., and notations thereon, signed by J. M. Settle and dated October 14 and October 24, 1863, in Robins Papers.

October 11, having exempted judicial and executive officers of both Confederate and state governments, had failed to exempt state officers declared by law to be liable to militia duty. There was resulting confusion, so the act was amended on April 30, 1863, to provide that state officers exempted by virtue of gubernatorial action because of the vital need for them in the administration of government should be exempted by the military authorities. Pursuant to this act, Vance exempted the militia officers of the state of North Carolina.

Kirk's counsel argued that the Governor had claimed exemption for certain officers and that this exemption continued until the adjournment of the next regular session of the legislature; he argued further that the Governor could not switch from one position to another, and that he could not take away exemptions from particular individuals in a class without removing all. Counsel for the Confederate States took the position that the Governor could claim exemptions as he saw fit, there being no requirement that he exempt by classes. Various orders, cited on both sides, seemingly supported the position taken by their respective introducers.

Judge Pearson reached the conclusion that the Governor's order did not have the effect of avoiding the exemption of Kirk and other militia officers of the two counties mentioned, that the General Assembly would decide which officers were needed for government, that Congress amended the exemption acts when the General Assembly was not in session, and that Congress did not plan to confer power on a governor to exempt state officers as this would be a deprivation of its own Congressional power. He felt that intention to make an act of Congress dependent on a governor's action was questionable, though such an interpretation had been upheld. The express provision of the law that any exemptions granted by the Governor were to be in effect only until after the adjournment of the next General Assembly was also considered. Pearson observed that there were dangers inherent in verbal orders; as a result of his opinion, Kirk was discharged.[59]

A constable, elected to office in March, 1863, entered upon the discharge of his duties. In April, he was sent to a camp of instruction, and on May 5, he entered the army. He served about six weeks, and though he did receive bounty, he did not receive pay. He then went home, pending a decision in his case. On January 15, 1864, he sued out a writ of habeas corpus. Under the act of May 1, 1863, providing for the exemption of all state officers claimed by the governor of a state for the due administration of government, the petitioner claimed exemption. Governor Vance had exempted, among others, constables who had entered into bond before May 11, 1863. In December, the legislature ratified the action. Judge Pearson ruled that acceptance of

[59] *In re* F. W. Kirk, 60 N.C. 186 (1863).

bounty was no waiver to his claim. He held further that absence from his duty did not deprive him of his office, as no legal proceeding had been initiated to deprive him of it. Finding no proviso which would exclude those in service from the application of the act relating to state officers, Pearson discharged the man.[60]

The question of exemptions for government officials became of more and more concern as the months passed. President Davis wrote to Governor Vance in July, 1863, discussing the enrollment of such persons in North Carolina. He referred to the provisions of the law which authorized him to interfere in cases of particular hardship with an order of special exemption, but he indicated that he could not exempt classes. So far as constables and justices of the peace were concerned, enrolling officers were ordered to suspend action until a conference could be held with Vance; but Davis said he did not consider it within his power to extend general exemption to the police of corporate towns, though policemen attached to the home guard might be permitted to remain at home. Davis assured Vance that the conscription officers had been instructed to enforce the laws rigidly only where necessary, and he hoped that differences between Confederate and state authorities could be resolved.[61]

Public office holding as a means of escape was the target of Randolph Abbott Shotwell. Writing of state elections, he expressed the opinion that the Confederacy should:

... recruit our armies with the thousands; and tens of thousands, yea *hundreds of thousands* of able-bodied men, who escape duty, live comfortably at home, and even by extortion on poor soldier's families, under the exempting plea of holding some petty office! It is really astonishing how many exempted persons there are in the South, despite all the talk about robbing the cradle and the grave. There are *above 5,000* "Magistrates" in Virginia, and North Carolina alone. There are nearly 2,000 members of the ["]Legislature" in the twelve Southern States, exclusive of Kentucky and Missouri. There are nearly 1,000 clerks of county court; nearly as many Registers of Deeds; and in most states a Judge-in-Chancery, or Equity-Clerk. Then there are countless petty officers (both State and Confederate) for gathering supplies, running mills, etc. Of course, a considerable number of these are very necessary. But it is equally true that the larger numbers are *not* actually necessary, while a great many are altogether unnecessary in a time of trouble, and want, and imminent peril such as now exists.[62]

Shotwell also referred to the thousands who escaped "sharing the trials and perils of the field simply because they are shrewd enough to secure some petty office." He added that he knew "*some* officials are

[60] In the Matter of Bradshaw, 60 N.C. 379 (1864).
[61] Jefferson Davis to Zebulon B. Vance, July 14, 1863, in *Official Records,* Series IV, II, 632-633.
[62] Hamilton, ed., *Shotwell Papers,* I, 470.

indispensable and many of them are filled by crippled or sickly soldiers, who were called to the duties by the cordial wish of their fellow citizens."[63]

The question of exemption for state officials was to become increasingly acute as the months passed, and many judicial interpretations in this area of the law occurred after the enactment of 1864 legislation.

Various technical matters were taken to the courts for rulings. One Austin had been exempted from the army because he had furnished a substitute, and he had also been exempted from militia duty. On September 15, 1863, the home guard members were ordered to arrest every deserter and recusant conscript. As Judge Pearson pointed out, such service by the home guard would naturally promote efficiency of the Confederate army, but it would also impose on exempt citizens a dangerous duty. He felt that the question had to be considered objectively, "unaffected by collateral considerations growing out of the condition of our country. . . ." This duty would be a natural function of the militia, and the Governor was authorized by law to require this type of duty from that group. The Court refused to permit the use of persons exempt from militia duty for this job. Judge Pearson spoke of the functions of the home guard, a body apart and distinct from the militia, made up of exempts and those persons over the age limits for service elsewhere. The guard members were given specific functions by law, and the Governor had no authority to order them to perform other duties. The Court reached the conclusion that the home guard was not responsible for service such as that to which Austin was ordered. The petitioner was discharged.[64]

The responsibility of persons not domiciled in North Carolina but living in the state to serve as members of the home guard was also discussed by the Court. One Finley, a native of Baltimore, decided to visit North Carolina in May, 1861, with the intention of remaining in the state for the duration of the war. When ordered into the home guard in October, 1863, he refused to go. Arguments were advanced in his behalf which stated that legislation regarding the home guard was unconstitutional because the regular army and the militia were the only military organizations recognized by the Confederacy, and that Finley was not domiciled in North Carolina but was a subject of a country with which the South was at war and was, therefore, an alien enemy. The North Carolina Supreme Court left unanswered the question of constitutionality, saying a decision on that point was not required in order to determine the outcome of the case at hand. Judge Pearson's opinion stated that the legislature intended to include in the law foreigners who had been residents of the state for thirty days, without reference to domicile. In this particular case, however, Finley could

---

[63] *Ibid.*, p. 471.
[64] *In re* Austin, 60 N.C. 168 (1863) and 60 N.C. 544 (1864).

not be regarded as a foreigner within the meaning of the law; rather, he was an alien enemy, remaining in the state by permission of its government. Indicating that a soldier had to be trusted and that an enemy alien might desert and reveal vital information, the Court held that the law did not imply that alien enemies were to be encompassed within its meaning. When the presence of such a person became a danger to the public safety, permission for him to reside in North Carolina would be withdrawn. In the meantime, Finley was granted a discharge.[65]

The variety and number of cases discussed are typical of a far greater number heard by the courts and by individual judges. The relative ease with which a disgruntled draftee could obtain release from military authorities became known throughout the Confederate Army. Dissatisfaction with life in camp and on the battle front was probably secondary to concern and worry about those at home, and many soldiers determined to obtain release legally rather than desert, though desertion was in itself a major problem. The fact that the North Carolina Supreme Court justices, particularly Chief Justice Richmond M. Pearson, granted writs of habeas corpus and subsequently released many from military service created dissension and consternation among the Confederate officials. The rulings of the Court strained relations between Governor Zebulon B. Vance, who felt it his duty to uphold the opinions of the Court, and the Confederate officials. With the State of North Carolina adhering to its doctrine of sovereignty for its own government, there was little the Confederate government could do but protest.

In an effort to change the picture, however, governmental and military authorities of the Confederacy knew that drastic action had to be taken to stem the tide of both public and judicial opinion. Such action occurred early in 1864 with the enactment of additional legislation by the Confederate Congress. Though changes in the law were intended to tighten matters relating to conscription and exemption, judicial review by the courts of North Carolina did not cease. Neither did the tendency of the Supreme Court to release men from service change after the passage of new and strict laws.

[65] *In re* Finley, 60 N.C. 191 (1863).

III

LEGISLATION AND LEGAL OPINIONS IN 1864

The numerous discharges resulting from the legal interpretations of the conscription and exemption acts, the attitude of the public toward conscription, and the setbacks suffered by the army all contributed to the concern of the Confederate officials. President Davis, addressing the Fourth Session of the First Congress, spoke on December 8, 1863, of the need for "restoring to the Army all who are improperly absent, putting an end to substitution, modifying the exemption law, restricting details, and placing in the ranks such of the able-bodied men now employed as wagoners, nurses, cooks, and other employees as are doing service for which the negroes may be found competent."[1]

The President elaborated on the policy of permitting the use of substitutes, saying that those men often deserted and that dissatisfaction resulted among those unable to avoid service by the procurement of a substitute. He agreed with the theory that a new provision, resulting in the call of those who had earlier furnished substitutes, would not be a breach of contract. Davis reasoned that acceptance by the government of a substitute was a privilege rather than a contractual arrangement. He recommended a drastic change in the system of exemptions, pointing out abuses in the methods then being followed. The policy of exempting those skilled in and engaged in essential occupations was sensible, but the same end could be obtained by conscripting such persons and allowing details to meet the needs of the country. Some duties could be performed by those above conscript age instead of details then assigned to such tasks. Davis felt that persons over forty-five could guard posts, bridges, and railroads, could apprehend deserters, and could perform other duties of a comparable nature.[2]

The Confederate Congress acted, and on December 28, 1863, that body provided that no person would thereafter be permitted to furnish a substitute and that no substitute would be received.[3] A further enactment, of January 5, 1864, provided that no person would be exempted from service because he had furnished a substitute. Those persons not liable to military service because of other reasons, who had sent substitutes, were not to be affected by the new law.[4]

[1] Message of Jefferson Davis to House and Senate, December 8, 1863, in Confederate States of America *Senate Journal*, 1 Cong., 4 Sess., 1863, p. 446.

[2] *Ibid.*

[3] *Confederate Laws*, 1 Cong., 4 Sess., 1863-1864, c. III.

[4] *Ibid.*, c. IV.

These changes, which conformed to the ideas advanced by the President, were not accepted with universal approval. One newspaper, discussing the position of Davis and Congress regarding the matter of a contract between the government and a principal, stated that there was indeed a repudiation of a contract when a man who had furnished a substitute was later called into service. The paper "had hoped that the Southern Confederacy would be a model of principle, and justice, and constancy."[5]

On February 3, 1864, Davis again addressed the Confederate Senate and House members, reminding the legislators that state courts and judges had impaired the efficiency of the army by issuing writs of habeas corpus and that a judge known for his tendency to discharge petitioners would find himself besieged with petitions. He pointed out the resulting inconvenience to military personnel and expressed the belief that questions involving the constitutionality of the acts of Congress which placed in service those who had furnished substitutes would undoubtedly increase. As a remedy, the President recommended the suspension of the writ of habeas corpus, in accordance with the provisions of the Constitution. Davis explained that such action would be "a sharp remedy, but a necessary one." He continued his address by saying:

It is a remedy plainly contemplated by the Constitution. . . . It may occasion some clamor; but this will proceed chiefly from the men who have already too long been the active spirits of evil. Loyal citizens will not feel danger, and the disloyal must be made to fear it. The very existence of extraordinary powers often renders their exercise unnecessary. To temporize with disloyalty in the midst of war is but to quicken it to the growth of treason. I, therefore, respectfully recommend that the privilege of the writ of habeas corpus be suspended.[6]

As far back as February, 1862, Congress had authorized the suspension of the writ when cities, towns, and military districts were in danger of attack and martial law was required.[7] In April[8] and again in October[9] Congress had passed additional legislation permitting the the suspension of the writ in limited situations and on a limited basis. These acts, however, were as nothing compared to that enacted on February 15, 1864, when the writ of habeas corpus was suspended in cases of treason, in cases of conspiracies to overthrow the government or resist Confederate authorities, in situations where people were

[5] Salisbury *Carolina Watchman*, January 4, 1864.

[6] Message of Jefferson Davis to House and Senate, February 3, 1864, Confederate States of America *Senate Journal*, 1 Cong., 4 Sess. (1863-1864), pp. 670-671.

[7] *Confederate Laws*, 1 Cong., 1 Sess., 1862, c. II.

[8] *Ibid.*, c. XLIV, ss. [1], 2.

[9] *Confederate Laws*, 1 Cong., 2 Sess., 1862, c. LI, ss. [1]-3.

combining to resist the enemy and incite insurrection, in cases of desertion or encouragement of desertion (with the proviso that in cases of wrong and oppression by a subordinate officer to a person who did not legally owe military service the superior officer was to give prompt relief), in actions involving spying, in matters involving unlawful trading with the enemy, in cases of conspiracies to liberate prisoners of war, and in conspiracies to aid the enemy, and also in other specified actions regarded as treasonable. The act was to be in force for ninety days following the succeeding meeting of Congress.[10]

Discussions of matters involving conscription were held in secret sessions.[11] Out of these discussions came significant legislation. On February 17, 1864, Congress provided that all white men of the Confederate States, between the ages of seventeen and fifty, were to serve in the armed forces.[12] Those between eighteen and forty-five then in service were to be retained during the war, though certain transfers from one company to another were permitted.[13] No person was to be relieved from the operation of the act because of previous discharge, except for disability, and those who had furnished substitutes were not to be exempted. Congress provided that those exempted on religious grounds who had paid the tax would be excused from military service.[14] Persons between seventeen and eighteen and between forty-five and fifty were to enroll; failure of men in those age groups to comply with the law would result in service in the field. Otherwise, they were to be used as a reserve for state defense and detail duty, and service away from their home states was not to be required.[15] Various details as to the operation of the law were outlined in the statutes.[16]

Perhaps the most significant section of the new law was that which repealed all previous laws granting exemptions. Those exemptions to be recognized under the new enactment included those unfit for military service; top Confederate and state officials and legislators and "such other Confederate and State officers as the President or the Governors of the respective States may certify to be necessary for the proper administration of the Confederate or State Governments. . ."; ministers regularly employed in the discharge of their duties; superintendents and physicians of asylums for the deaf, dumb, blind, and insane; one editor for each newspaper and those employees certified by him to be indispensable; the public printer of the Confederate and state governments, and such journeymen printers as might be indispensable;

[10] *Confederate Laws*, 1 Cong., 4 Sess., 1863-1864, c. XXXVII.
[11] See Confederate States of America, *House Journal* and *Senate Journal*, 1 Cong., 4 Sess. (1863-1864), *passim*.
[12] *Confederate Laws*, 1 Cong., 4 Sess., 1863-1864, c. LXV, [s. 1].
[13] *Ibid.*, s. 2.
[14] *Ibid.*, s. 4.
[15] *Ibid.*, s. 5.
[16] *Ibid.*, ss. 3, 6, 7, 8, 9, 12.

one apothecary for each such store, provided he was doing business on October 10, 1862, and had continued in business since that date; physicians over thirty years of age who had been practicing for seven years, but excluding dentists; presidents and teachers of colleges, seminaries, academies, and schools who had been engaged in their duties for two years before the passage of the act, with the added proviso that the school should have a minimum of twenty students; superintendents of public hospitals established by law prior to the passage of the act, and those physicians and nurses as were indispensable to the efficient management of those hospitals; one overseer for plantations meeting specified conditions outlined in the statute, including the provision that such exempted person was to execute a bond to secure the delivery of certain produce to the government; various railroad officials and employees; and mail contractors and hack and coach drivers for mail as specified in the act passed in April, 1863.[17] The President was authorized to grant details under general rules of the War Department and under specified provisos set forth by Congress.[18]

On the same date, Congress made able-bodied free Negroes liable for the performance of duties which they could advantageously perform. Negro slaves were also to be used for similar duties, though not over twenty thousand were to be so employed, and the owners were to receive wages for their use.[19]

Even before the passage of the acts, the newspapers carried various articles on impending legislation and rumors pertaining thereto. In January, the *Carolina Watchman* quoted the *Western Sentinel*, which explained the meaning of the suspension of the writ of habeas corpus, saying it did not favor such action, though it was not believed that liberties would be endangered if representatives in Congress felt such a step to be needed.[20] The Raleigh *Standard* told its readers that no decision had been made by the courts concerning the constitutionality of the law suspending the writ of habeas corpus, but that the belief seemed to be generally held that the act would be found to be unconstitutional. The paper observed that the decision of one judge in vacation in a habeas corpus case was as binding as that of another and that every such decision was binding as law until reversed by the full Supreme Court. A bill to authorize a special term of court having failed to pass, the paper expressed the hope that the judges would meet on their own initiative and make a joint decision regarding the matter. The newspaper also reported that Governor Vance had "pledged his

[17] *Ibid.*, s. 10.
[18] *Ibid.*, s. 11.
[19] *Ibid.*, c. LXXIX, ss. [1], 2.
[20] Salisbury *Carolina Watchman*, January 25, 1864, quoting the *Western Sentinel*.

word to enforce the decision of our State judiciary, and we believe he will do it."[21]

Another paper reported that Alabama had passed an act making the denial of the writ of habeas corpus a felony, and it commented with favor on the action. "Dark as is the situation of the country, it is surely not yet necessary to convert the Government into a despotism in order to retrieve its fortunes.... Let it not be said of us that we threw off one tyranny only to build up another at home."[22] The *Standard* reported that Vance had spoken in Wilkesboro of his regret with regard to the action, but he had said the law had to be enforced. In a speech at Hendersonville, the Governor had expressed his horror of martial law, pointing out the fact that the suspension of the writ of habeas corpus was a deprivation of one single right while martial law suspended all civil law.[23]

A Richmond paper, in an article on the extension of the conscription law, reported that officers in Lee's army opposed the inclusion of men over forty-five because of the probability of short supplies. The paper expressed the opinion that the primary discontent in the army stemmed from the policy of permitting substitutes, indicating that "in a majority of cases, substitutes deserted, while such as remained were found generally inefficient."[24]

Following passage of the new legislation, General Order 33 was issued, on March 15, ordering the Bureau of Conscription to enroll all between seventeen and eighteen and between forty-five and fifty years of age.[25] A circular issued from the Conscript Office in Raleigh on March 28, by order of Peter Mallett, outlined the procedure to be followed. Minute investigation was to be made of all claims for exemption or detail. The Commandant indicated his trust in the enrolling officers to meet their new duties with "the zeal, patriotism and energy, which have hitherto been evinced in their efforts in our great cause, and to execute these duties with firmness tempered by discretion."[26]

Enforcement of the 1864 enactments met with resistance. Governor Vance wrote to the Secretary of War, asking for suspension of the execution of the conscription law in western North Carolina because

[21] Raleigh *Standard*, January 29, 1864.

[22] Salisbury *Carolina Watchman*, February 15, 1864, quoting the *South Carolinian*.

[23] Raleigh *Standard*, July 13, 1864.

[24] Salisbury *Carolina Watchman*, February 8, 1864, quoting the Richmond *Whig*.

[25] General Orders No. 33, issued by General Samuel Cooper, Adjutant and Inspector General, March 15, 1864, in *Official Records*, Series IV, III, 212.

[26] Circular No. 10, issued from Conscript Office, Raleigh, by order of Colonel Peter Mallett, signed by E. J. Hardin, Adjutant, March 28, 1864, copy filed in record of Murdoch White v. Peter Mallett, 1864, in Original Supreme Court Papers.

of conditions there.[27] Endorsements on the letter and the reply to Vance indicated that there was doubt on the part of the War Department as to the wisdom of yielding to the dissatisfied people, and that President Davis concurred in the answer.[28] After conferring with Col. Mallett, Thomas H. Holmes reported in April, 1864, that he was "pained to report that there is much disaffection in many of the counties, which, emboldened by the absence of troops, is being organized in some places to resist enrolling officers. . . ."[29]

Individuals sought favored status for themselves by various means. One man wrote to Marmaduke Robins, private secretary to Governor Vance, asking him to send exemption papers to the Governor and obtain consent for the applicant to spend the winter in Florida or some southern place. He said he made the request only because of "imperative necessity."[30]

Far more common than individual appeals to influential persons was resort to legal action. As had been true in interpreting the laws of 1862 and 1863, Judge Pearson was again the central figure in these decisions, and was consequently the subject of much correspondence between Governor Vance and the Confederate officials.

Not unexpected were questions involving the interpretation of the law suspending the writ of habeas corpus. General Orders Number 31, issued from Richmond on March 10, 1864, after quoting the act of Congress, explained that after a person who had been enlisted in the army or in a unit for local defense applied for a writ of habeas corpus the officer having custody of the person was to report the case with all relevant facts to the War Department. That Department would, in turn, furnish the proper answer to be made to the writ, and the person applying was to be kept in custody under this order. A copy of the order was to be sent to the officer in court issuing the writ. Where delay could not be obtained, the officer in command was to make a special return in writing indicating that the person was being detained by authority of the Secretary of War, and he was to decline to produce the body as demanded in the writ.[31]

In view of the major legislation, followed by military orders, of the early months of 1864, court action was not surprising. The leading

[27] Zebulon B. Vance to James A. Seddon, April 11, 1864, in *Official Records*, Series I, LIII, 324.

[28] Endorsements on Vance to Seddon letter, cited above, p. 325, and Seddon to Vance, April 23, 1864, in *Official Records*, Series I, LIII, 329.

[29] Thomas H. Holmes to Samuel Cooper, April 29, 1864, in *Official Records*, Series IV, III, 353.

[30] J. A. C. Zournal? [name not clear] to Marmaduke Robins, December 3, 1864, in Robins Papers.

[31] General Orders No. 31, issued from the Adjutant and Inspector General's Office in Richmond, March 10, 1864, signed by Samuel Cooper, in *Official Records*, Series IV, III, 203-205.

North Carolina case resulting from the habeas corpus enactments was soon before the courts. Walton v. Gatlin involved a man who had applied to Judge Pearson on January 27, 1864, for a writ of habeas corpus, alleging his legal exemption rights. The writ was granted at the request of Walton, despite a return by T. H. Gatlin, a captain who had the petitioner in his custody, stating that Walton should serve because of the act of Congress, passed January 5, 1864, which made principals liable even when they had previously furnished substitutes. Walton was, however, discharged by Judge Pearson on February 19. Gatlin then moved for a writ of certiorari, directed to the Chief Justice, commanding him to certify to the Supreme Court the record involving the writ of habeas corpus issued by him and his judgment thereon. As the counsel for the Confederacy had indicated his intention to take such action at the time of the original hearing, the Chief Justice had bound Walton for appearance in the Supreme Court. Walton's counsel argued that the action of a single judge in vacation on a writ of habeas corpus was not the subject of review, but the certiorari was granted and the case went to the full Court.

Commenting on the conflicts in the opinions, Judge Pearson distinguished a habeas corpus issued when a person was committed for crime from a habeas corpus resulting from imprisonment or restraint of liberty for some other reason. He reviewed the procedure followed in cases of commitment, showing that the examining magistrate reviewed the case and made the decision. The logical conclusion to this type of hearing was that no review by certiorari was possible because there had been no trial. On the other hand, a writ of habeas corpus issued because of restraint of liberty for other than crime was determined by a judgment, which was the subject of review. The jurisdiction to hear such cases being extended to judges in vacation and to a single judge did not preclude the full Court from possessing the same jurisdictional powers. Action taken by Superior courts and by judges in vacation could be reviewed without question, according to Pearson. He pointed out the necessity for the full Court's having the power of review; without it, one man would serve because of the decision of one judge while another would be exempted because of the ruling of another judge. Judge Battle concurred with the Chief Justice; but Judge Manly dissented, feeling that the Supreme Court had no right, at common law or by statute, to revise a decision made at chambers by a writ of error, recordari, or other legal process.[32]

The right to carry the issue up on a writ of certiorari having been granted, Gatlin pursued his action. The habeas corpus petition showed that the Congress had, on January 5, 1864, ended exemptions for those who had furnished substitutes. The question of constitutionality of

[32] Edward S. Walton v. T. H. Gatlin, 60 N.C. 310 (1864).

that act was put before the Court. Judge Pearson had reasoned that the petitioner, by furnishing a substitute under the act of April 16, 1862, had entered into a binding contract with the government—a contract which Congress had no power to violate. In a long opinion, in which he reviewed the history of governmental power in England and in early America, Judge Battle concluded that the Confederate government had the right of eminent domain and the power of commanding the services of citizens capable of bearing arms, and that the act of January 5 was, therefore, constitutional. If indeed a contract was made in April, 1862, the government had the right to annul such a contract when the necessity of the country so demanded. The party lacking the right to annul the contract knew when he entered into it that the other party, the government, did possess such power. The fact that the constitutionality of the act had been upheld by courts of Virginia, Georgia, and Alabama was cited by Judge Battle. Concurring with him was Judge Manly, who argued that if a contract had existed, it was a contract subject to conditions. Congress, in the exercise of its war power, could not grant permanent exemptions, and the act of April, 1862, did not authorize exemptions as a matter of contract but as a matter of grace. Manly specifically stated that the act was constitutional.[33]

With two of the three judges of the Supreme Court agreeing, Judge Pearson's opinion, rendered in vacation, was reversed and Walton was surrendered to Gatlin. In his dissenting opinion, Judge Pearson reiterated his belief that there had been no error in his judgment at Salisbury, that his colleagues on the bench had based their opinions on the ground that " 'necessity knows no law' "; and that no government could violate its own contract without believing in the principle that " 'might makes right.' " Judge Pearson spoke feelingly for his position.[34]

The Walton case was carried in detail on the front page of the *Carolina Watchman*.[35] The same paper, a week or so later, quoted the Wilmington *Journal* which had said that in no case before him had Judge Pearson failed to decide against the Confederacy. "So uniform has been his course, so well known and decided are his proclivities, that, no matter what the case may be, the public are always prepared for the same result—a decision against the Confederate Government." The *Watchman* answered the Wilmington paper by quoting from the Fayetteville *Observer*, which had observed that it could not reconcile the inconsistency of some of his decisions, but in fairness to Judge Pearson, it wanted to point out that of the first thirty-five cases before

[33] T. H. Gatlin v. Edward S. Walton, 60 N.C. 325 (1864) and *Ex Parte* Walton, 60 N.C. 350 (1864), which is treated as if it were part of the Gatlin v. Walton case. See also records in Original Supreme Court Papers.

[34] T. H. Gatlin v. Edward S. Walton, 60 N.C. 325 at 349 (1864).

[35] Salisbury *Carolina Watchman*, February 29, 1864.

him, seven had been decided in favor of the Confederacy. The paper was unaware of the statistics on later decisions.[36]

After the decision by the full court in the Walton case, one newspaper commented on Judge Battle's decision and said that the opinion "enforces the just conception of a government in its strength and majesty, able to protect its subjects, and to command them for their and its protection. . . ."[37]

Before the opinion of the full Court had been given, Governor Vance wrote to James A. Seddon concerning difficulties arising from conscription of principals of substitutes in North Carolina. In his letter, he commented on Judge Pearson's decision regarding the constitutionality of the act. He also referred to the fact that the Chief Justice was continuing to grant the writ, despite conflicts with state and Confederate authorities. Vance took the position that the discharge of a single individual by a judge in chambers was not binding except as to that particular man, but he felt he would have to protect a discharged man until the meeting of the full Supreme Court in June. He requested that the enrollment of principals be stopped temporarily, stating that Judge Pearson and the counsel for the Confederacy had agreed to carry one case on certiorari to the full Court. Though such an arrangement might deprive the Confederacy of the services of men until June, the peace between the two governments would be preserved. Making no comment on Judge Pearson's decision, the Governor observed that the laws of the Confederacy were at the mercy of the several judges of the various states. He commented that obedience to judges was preferable to the assumption of judicial power by the executive branch of the government.[38]

Seddon replied that he, too, would like to avoid misunderstanding, but that the decision of Judge Pearson on the constitutionality of the law "appears, to my humble judgment, strange and clearly incorrect . . ." and that the enrolling officers would proceed with their duty. Recognizing the legality of Judge Pearson's decision, pending reversal, he said no effort would be made to arrest a man discharged by the Judge, but there was no reason to suspend enrollment.[39]

President Davis also agreed that the law would have to be enforced in North Carolina as elsewhere, though he agreed that Pearson's decision would be respected pending the outcome of the appeal. He felt certain, however, that there would be a reversal.[40]

[36] *Ibid.*, March 14, 1864, including quotations from the Wilmington *Journal* and the Fayetteville *Observer*.

[37] *Ibid.*, July 25, 1864, quoting the *Confederate*.

[38] Zebulon B. Vance to James A. Seddon, February 29, 1864, in *Official Records*, Series IV, III, 176-177.

[39] Seddon to Vance, March 5, 1864, in *Official Records*, Series IV, III, 197-198.

[40] Jefferson Davis to Thomas Bragg, March 7, 1864, in *Official Records*, Series IV, III, 200-201.

On March 12, the Secretary of War wrote to Thomas Bragg to ask if he would assume responsibility as chief commissioner for duties arising under the habeas corpus act.[41] Bragg replied that he did not want the job, but he would accept. In his reply he referred to a letter from Judge Pearson relative to the question of constitutionality of the act suspending the writ of habeas corpus in the case of a person attempting to avoid military service. Bragg indicated that the letter had been written prior to the published decision by Judge Battle, refusing to grant a writ where it appeared on the face of the petition that the applicant was attempting to avoid service. Having heard that Judge Manly had taken the same course of action, Bragg expressed the hope that Pearson would "not persist in his course."[42] When he wrote to express pleasure at learning of Bragg's acceptance, Seddon added:

Judge Pearson is still, I fear, bent on mischief. It will be hard, however, for him to prevent by construction the plain terms of the law, or to stem alone the changing current of public sentiment and the adverse opinions of his brethren on the bench. He will probably find discretion the better policy, and for a time at least, and, I trust, permanently, cloak his factious purposes.[43]

Bragg wrote in late March, referring to 115 or 120 of the "Salisbury cases," similar to the original case heard by Judge Pearson in that town.[44] Seddon, writing in turn to Bragg, said there had been no orders other than General Orders Number 31, providing that the War Department would not prevent litigation when a bona fide case arose. The Department wanted to keep those desiring to evade service "from availing themselves of the crude opinions and injurious efforts of some judges who seem to have come to the conclusion that by diminishing the Army and obstructing the authority of Congress they are performing a public duty."[45]

Shortly before and during the period of this correspondence, Judge Pearson heard numerous petitions for writs of habeas corpus. He had gone so far as to discharge a man in December, 1863, who had actually served sixteen months after being enrolled. The fellow had, before the passage of the conscript act, placed a substitute in for the war and had been discharged. Later, despite his discharge, the man was enrolled, and he served for a time. When he went home on sick leave and refused to return to the army, he was arrested. During his service, he had received clothing and pay but no bounty. The enrolling officer, relying on the early case of Hamilton C. Graham, contended that the

[41] James A. Seddon to Thomas Bragg, March 12, 1864, in *Official Records*, Series IV, III, 210.
[42] Bragg to Seddon, March 15, 1864, in *Official Records*, Series IV, III, 213.
[43] Bragg to Seddon, March 19, 1864, in *Official Records*, Series IV, III, 238.
[44] Bragg to Seddon, March 29, 1864, in *Official Records*, Series IV, III, 256.
[45] Seddon to Bragg, April 2, 1864, in *Official Records*, Series IV, III, 267.

offense of absence without leave had to be disposed of by a court-martial before any other question could be argued. Judge Pearson showed that Graham had been arrested for a collateral offense and had enlisted in the army, whereas the petitioner then before him had been forced into the army against his will. The petitioner was not liable to conscription, the enrolling officer had refused to exempt him because he had been instructed to disregard Supreme Court decisions unless the party had been discharged on a writ of habeas corpus, and the man had not waived his right to exemption merely by serving sixteen months. Pearson determined that the government should not be permitted to take advantage of its own wrong, as it was trying to do. The Judge stated the petitioner had had to draw pay in order to support himself and his family, but he had received no bounty and the months served were regarded by Pearson as being sufficient time extracted from the petitioner. Basing his decision on the reasons he had set out and distinguishing the case from others, Judge Pearson granted a discharge.[46]

On December 27, 1863, Judge Pearson wrote to his colleague, Judge Battle, giving him his reasoning and explaining the way in which he had distinguished the Graham case from others. He began the letter to his fellow-judge by referring to the "fortunate" situation which existed in that he and Battle had as "seldom differed in our conclusions, as any two Judges ever did who sat together as long." He remarked that each of them had " 'a single eye to the truth.' "[47] That Pearson felt it necessary to write such a letter, defending his position, is indicative of his conscientiousness in rendering decisions known to him to be contrary to the thinking of many individuals and officials. Despite his minority position, however, the Chief Justice continued to state his belief in the right of a person to petition for the writ of habeas corpus, be heard, and be discharged if the facts warranted release.[48]

In a detailed opinion handed down in May, 1864, Judge Pearson again reviewed the question of habeas corpus and legislation pertaining thereto. One Cain, who had put in a substitute for the war, was arrested by the enrolling officer. An appeal to the officer produced no results, so Cain asked for a special writ directed to the sheriff. Pearson reasoned that if the act suspending the writ of habeas corpus covered this case, and if Congress possessed the right to suspend the writ by legislation, the petitioner would not be entitled to a special writ, which would be tantamount to doing indirectly what could not be done directly.

[46] In the Matter of William Wyrick, 60 N.C. 375 (1864). Though reported in 1864, the decision was rendered in December, 1863.

[47] Richmond M. Pearson to William H. Battle, December 27, 1863, in Pearson Papers.

[48] See, for example, petitions of David Jordan, February 22, 1864, and Thomas Jordan, February 22, 1864, in Guilford County Papers, and In the Matter of Roseman, 60 N.C. 368 (1864).

Deciding that the petitioner had applied for a civil remedy to assert a private right under a contract and that the petitioner was not charged with a crime, the Chief Justice decided that Cain was entitled to the special writ.

In his opinion, the history of various types of writs was reviewed in detail. Included in the discussion were those issued when a person stood committed or detained as a prisoner for crime, those for a civil cause when a person was restrained of liberty for other than a criminal offense, and those issued to bring a prisoner in to testify, as well as other lesser known writs and their uses. Pearson concluded that Congress only suspended the writ of habeas corpus *ad subjiciendum*, used when a person stood committed or detained as a prisoner for crime, and that the suspension did not include other writs. The Constitutional clause giving Congress power to suspend the writ referred only to this first type of writ, according to the reasoning of the Chief Justice. Going back into English constitutional history and early American history, the Judge discussed the historical and legal development of the meaning of the writ of habeas corpus. He questioned the power of Congress to pass an act and subsequently make it a crime to apply for a civil remedy to test the constitutionality of that act. Believing that the petitioner was detained because he applied for a writ of habeas corpus, Pearson determined that he was entitled to the special writ for which he petitioned.[49]

A few months earlier, Judge Battle had been faced with a comparable case. One M. Long had also argued that the suspension of the writ of habeas corpus was an unconstitutional action. In his opinion, Battle stated that the constitutionality of the act could not be questioned, that the law was binding on all judges, that various cases in which the act was suspended were outlined in the statute, and that one of the applicable situations in which the act was to be suspended was concerned with persons who attempted to avoid military service. The argument was advanced that the act was to apply only to persons liable to service who were attempting to avoid it, not to those seeking the benefit of the writ solely to establish their claim to exemption. Battle interpreted such a construction as being so restrictive as to defeat the purpose of the law. The Judge pointed out the fact that the law provided a remedy for those who did not legally owe military service in that a procedure was established whereby a superior officer could give redress when a person was wronged by a subordinate. At the time of his opinion, Judge Battle said he was aware of the decision of Judge Pearson in the Walton case and others, but he was not informed as to the reasoning advanced in those cases. Battle declined to issue the writ.[50]

[49] In the Matter of Cain, 60 N.C. 525 (1864).
[50] In the Matter of M. Long, 60 N.C. 534 (1864).

Judge Manly, too, handed down decisions during this period in which the Court did not sit as a body. Considering the Constitutional provision giving Congress power to suspend the writ only in the event of rebellion or invasion or when the public safety required it, Manly said that with the states invaded "from all quarters by the public enemy," such an occasion had indeed arisen. Consequently, he determined the act of Congress suspending the writ of habeas corpus to be constitutional, and the petitioner before him was remanded to the custody of the military authorities.[51]

In April, still during the period of vacation, Judge Pearson found that a return merely stating that the petitioner was detained under orders of the Secretary of War was so vague as to be comparable to no certificate. Ruling that there had to be an appearance in both civil and criminal cases, he determined that he could render no judgment because the certificate gave him nothing on which to act.[52]

The decision was in line with the reasoning of the Chief Justice as outlined in the letter to Judge Battle mentioned above. The preceding winter, he had expressed doubt as to the validity of habeas corpus cases heard on deposition. He felt that where there was a disputed fact, all cases required the witnesses to be present in person and notice to be given to the enrolling officers.[53]

The diversity of interpretation added to the confusion existing in the state with regard to the conscription and exemption laws and the act suspending the writ of habeas corpus. Several cases, in addition to the Walton case, were taken to the full Supreme Court by writ of certiorari. Such a case was that of one Trull, who had gone as a substitute from Haywood County in June, 1861. He served until the middle of April, 1864, when his principal, a man named Johnson, was conscripted. Trull then asked to be discharged on the ground that he was over fifty years of age, but his request was refused. The question to be settled was whether or not a substitute who had entered service as a result of the provisions of the April, 1862, act was entitled to a discharge upon the conscription of the principal after the passage of the act of January 5, 1864. The Court decided that the act of the government, in calling out the principal, did not end the liability of the substitute. No provision having been made for the discharge of substitutes by the act of January, these men were left in as volunteers. Concluding that the object of the act was to obtain additional men, the full Court reversed the opinion rendered in the chambers by Judge Pearson, and the petitioner was ordered to remain in service.[54]

[51] In the Matter of P. Rafter, 60 N.C. 536 (1864).
[52] In the Matter of Spivey, 60 N.C. 540 (1864).
[53] Richmond M. Pearson to William H. Battle, December 27, 1863, in Pearson Papers.
[54] Joseph McDaniel v. Trull, 60 N.C. 399 (1864).

Judicial interpretation having been given with regard to the writ of habeas corpus and the legislation affecting substitutes, the Court was then faced with other unanswered questions resulting from Congressional action of early 1864. Numerous cases arose under the act of February 17. Several decisions involved the age of persons enrolled. A writ of certiorari was sued out by Captain John M. Brawley to review a decision of Judge Pearson on a writ of habeas corpus. The petitioner, Tobias Kesler, had been enrolled under the act of February 17 as a senior reserve, his age at the time being between forty-five and fifty. After he reached the age of fifty, in October, 1864, he was discharged. Judge Battle concurred in the Pearson decision favoring discharge. The majority opinion held that white men between the ages of seventeen and fifty were to be in military service, that when a man passed out of this age group he was to be released and when he passed into this group he was to be conscripted. The number reaching seventeen compared to the number reaching fifty was about fifteen to one. Judge Manly's dissenting opinion spoke of the term of service, as outlined in the statute, being "for the war." Arguing that proof of birth was vague in many instances and that the army would be in a position of having to adjudicate cases daily under the majority interpretation, Manly felt that Congress could not have intended to limit service and that Congress had made no provision for discharge for any reason except disability.[55]

A related case involved a man who enrolled and who was arrested for duty in the army rather than as a senior reserve, after he had reached the age of forty-five. He was discharged from the army, though he was subject to call for duty in the senior reserves.[56]

The *Carolina Watchman* reported that it believed "the Supreme Court has decided that all men arriving at the venerable age of 50 should be dismissed.... Are there not some still held, who are rather an incumbrance than benefit to the army? They can do much good at home on their farms."[57]

Special Order Number 12, dated April 13, 1864, had ordered the enrollment of all between seventeen and eighteen and between forty-five and fifty; those persons were allowed until April 16 to join any company for local defense which might be formed.[58] These and similar orders[59]

[55] Tobias Kesler v. John M. Brawley, 60 N.C. 402 (1864).

[56] Miles Goodson v. J. D. Caldwell, 60 N.C. 519 (1864), and in Original Supreme Court Papers. See also *In re* Horton, Wake County, 1864, in Original Supreme Court Papers, in which a similar interpretation was given.

[57] Salisbury *Carolina Watchman*, November 21, 1864.

[58] Special Order No. 12, T. R. Emery to Col.[?] Foust, April 13, 1864, in Robins Papers. (An intensive search has failed to produce the given name of Foust.)

[59] See, for example, order from William F. Foushee to Marmaduke Robins, April 19, 1864, in Robins Papers.

resulted in a newspaper comment that "enrolling officers are about starting on another round. They seem determined to get the last available man. Let no one blame these officers, for they are simply sent out as the agents of the law, and can do no less than obey orders."[60]

Though "determined to get the last available man," the military authorities still found that numbers continued to resort to court action as a means of avoiding the application of the law to them. A long case involved Peter J. Sinclair, of Cumberland County, who edited the Fayetteville *North Carolinian*. Sinclair had suspended the paper temporarily when he entered military service in 1861. Late in December, 1863, he resumed publication after resigning his commission; the first issue of his paper appeared February 4, 1864. Sinclair was arrested as a conscript and petitioned for a writ of habeas corpus on August 12, 1864. The record is full of correspondence, including much between the North Carolina conscript officials and the Bureau of Conscription in Richmond. The facts revealed that the petitioner had applied for exemption as an editor on December 15, 1863, but his application had been refused. Appeals were sent to Governor Vance after the act of February 17 had exempted one editor for each paper, and Vance had recommended to the Bureau that Sinclair be permitted to continue the paper. Judges Battle and Manly concurred in the Supreme Court opinion which held that Sinclair was actually in military service at the time he became an editor, and the exemption provision of the act of February was not intended to apply to a person who was enrolled in service at the time it was enacted into law. As might be expected, Judge Pearson dissented.[61]

On the other hand, William G. Upchurch was discharged. He had worked off and on for the editor of the Raleigh *Standard*, and at the time of the passage of the February 17 act, he had asked for exemption and had obtained postponement regarding his case until May. He was then ordered to camp, but he appealed to the Board of Conscription and was permitted to remain at his employment until August. When ordered to report, he petitioned for a writ of habeas corpus, which was granted by the Chief Justice. The return showed that the petitioner had earlier furnished a substitute and had been exempted by Judge Battle in 1863, that he did not enroll under the February law, but that he did obtain employment with the *Standard* on May 2. An affidavit from the editor certified as to the essential nature of his work and indicated that he was not enrolled at the time he was employed. The Bureau of Conscription felt that the man's status on February 17 was the determining factor, holding that he was indeed enrolled at that time because of the requirements of the law. Judge Pearson, at Richmond

[60] Salisbury *Carolina Watchman*, May 2, 1864.
[61] *In re* Peter J. Sinclair, Cumberland County, 1864, in Original Supreme Court Papers.

Hill, discharged Upchurch and the case went to the Supreme Court on a writ of certiorari. There, Judge Manly agreed that February 17 fixed the status of each person so far as age was concerned and that the act was not *per se* an enrollment. He found that there was nothing to prevent a man from accepting an office provided he did so before being called into service, and his interpretation of the law stated that exemptions applied to employees in newspaper establishments at the time the act was passed as well as to those who might take the place of such persons or become necessary with the growth of the business. Since Upchurch was not called at the time his employment began, and had been certified as a necessary employee, he was exempted and Judge Pearson's opinion was affirmed.[62]

Numerous problems confronted both the military authorities and the home population because of the shortage of manpower. Decisions as to the greatest need for the services of skilled workers had to be made. For example, railroad employees were badly needed to keep the roads in repair, just as millers and blacksmiths were needed to supply the army and the people at home. The matter of details for the railroads in North Carolina was discussed in the summer of 1864, when the impossibility of operating and keeping the railroads in repair with the quota of one man per mile as allowed by law was stressed in a letter to the Quartermaster-General.[63] The Bureau of Conscription was requested to allow necessary details, but various endorsements on the letter indicated that the number of exempts was sufficient and that additional labor should be obtained elsewhere. A reduction in the number of details was proposed—one fourth at the end of thirty days, and an eighth at the end of every succeeding fifteen days until the number of employees was within the limits recognized by law.[64]

People skilled in various trades were vital to production at home, but at the same time, soldiers were badly needed. Numbers of the artisans, who preferred working at their trades to serving in the army, sought exemption through appeals to the courts. A miller who had been exempted was again enrolled in March, after passage of the February 17 act. A second time he was given a certificate of exemption. Though he reached the age of forty-five in May, he was ordered to camp on June 10; this time, his application for detail as a miller was refused. The result was a suit for a writ of habeas corpus. Holding that exemption after passage of the act of February 17 could only act as a furlough or detail, because the amended act repealed exemptions in such cases, the Court found that the status of the petitioner was

[62] William G. Upchurch v. S. W. Scott, 60 N.C. 520 (1864), and record in Original Supreme Court Papers.

[63] F. W. Sims to A. R. Lawton, August 16, 1864, in *Official Records*, Series IV, III, 598.

[64] Endorsements on letter from Sims to Lawton, cited above, pp. 599-600.

properly fixed as a soldier at the time of enrollment and detail, before he reached the age of forty-five. As a result of the decision, the petitioner was remanded.[65]

A consistent decision was reached in a case in which a man who had been an exempted blacksmith was enrolled on October 21, 1864. The question of his age entered the picture, and the Court held that the act of February 17 made all between seventeen and eighteen and between forty-five and fifty liable in the reserves. Had the man been between eighteen and forty-five at the time of enrollment, he would have been rightfully ordered into the army; being enrolled only after reaching forty-five, he was deemed to be liable for senior reserve duty only.[66]

Several decisions were made with regard to the exemption rights of mail carriers under the 1864 laws. A leading case involved Matthew Johnson, a man who had originally petitioned for detail as a farmer but had been turned down. He then claimed exemption as driver of a mail coach, having obtained such employment the day before he was ordered to go to camp. Judge Pearson released the man in September, but the Supreme Court opinion, written by Judge Battle, showed that the act of February 17 expressly stated that the act of April, 1863, was not repealed. Mail contractors and stage drivers were exempted; but Judge Battle held that the exemption was applicable only to men not enrolled at the time they assumed responsibilities as mail contractors or stage drivers, and that Congress did not intend to exempt a person from military duty to perform a job which could be as well done by another. The decision thereby reversed that of Judge Pearson.[67] The Chief Justice had gone so far as to release a petitioner who had bid on the job of carrying mail while he was in service, reasoning that the Post Office Department had called for bids without excluding those in military service from bidding, though the War Department had said those enrolled and those in service should not bid. As there was no proviso in the law to except those in service from participating in the bidding, Judge Pearson held that a bidder who had entered his bid and had been awarded the contract while in service was entitled to exemption.[68] The lack of unanimity in reasoning was again illustrated by these decisions.

Numerous cases resulted from the provisions of the February act with regard to overseers. One petitioner was deemed to be too late in applying for detail because he had waited nine months after passage of the act. The Court reasoned that the applicant could have sold his

[65] Edwin Haswell v. Peter Mallett, 60 N.C. 432 (1864).
[66] Miles Goodson v. J. D. Caldwell, 60 N.C. 519 (1864).
[67] Matthew Johnson v. Peter Mallett, 60 N.C. 511 (1864), and record in Original Supreme Court Papers.
[68] In the Matter of Jesse Sowers, 60 N.C. 384 (1864).

produce during the interval, thereby depriving the government of produce as specified in the law. Judge Pearson interpreted the tardiness as being a bar to favorable action on the petition.[69] Where a man had paid the five hundred dollars required by the act of May 1, 1863, which exempted one person for each farm owned by a *feme sole* under specified conditions, the Court concluded that he had fulfilled the terms of a contract with the government and was, therefore, entitled to exemption for the full period of twelve months covered by the bond. A Superior Court Judge, Robert B. Gilliam, rendered the decision, commenting on the fact that he had learned from Judge Pearson of his similar reasoning in a case presenting comparable facts.[70]

Interpretation of the law by the military authorities led to ludicrous conclusions at times. In one situation, the military officers decided that an old man eighty years old could serve as overseer, thereby precluding from exemption his son. The boy's father-in-law wrote to Marmaduke Robins seeking his intervention. The facts concerning the old man would have probably made an impact, but the writer went further. He expressed hope that Robins would use his influence

...in securing a position free from exposure of camp life as his health is very Delicate when Exposed in the least which frequently occurs. Friend Robbins [*sic*] this seems to be asking too much but my word for it you shall be rewarded & never forgotton [*sic*] for the favor. Joseph is a verry delicate man when exposed & I have no Idea that he will be of any service to the Confederate Govt. if exposed to camp life being subject to neuralga [*sic*] [.] Joseph is a man of verry fair Education with little Experience would be competent to assist in small department[.] Mr. Robbins if you can secure any position Please Reply forthwith to Dr Geo. K. Foust Greensboro in charge of Way Side Hospital.[71]

The fact that "Joseph is a verry delicate man when exposed" makes one wonder if he could have performed the overseer's job proficiently if he had been exempted by the military officials!

Another overseer attempted exemption from the home guard, alleging that he had filed his bond, which was approved, and qualified for exemption under the act of February 17. Despite this, he was ordered to report to Goldsboro for service in the home guard. The officer's return indicated that the petitioner, Bradshaw, was liable under North Carolina legislation; Bradshaw argued that by virtue of exemption from the army he was also exempt from home guard service. Judge Battle reviewed the legal obligation of those exempted under the law relating to overseers to furnish a required quota of provisions. Dissatisfaction

[69] Murdoch White v. Peter Mallett, 60 N.C. 430 (1864).

[70] Petition of John Q. McDougald, 1864, in Cumberland County Papers. A similar case, in which the McDougald decision was cited as a precedent, was *In re* John S. Shaw, 1864, also in Cumberland County Papers.

[71] George A. Foust to Marmaduke Robins, October 6, 1864, in Robins Papers.

with the earlier law showed that Congress intended, by the 1864 act, to place the bonded exempts in service as producers. The support of the armies obviously being necessary, the Court concluded that Congress acted within its authority in granting such exemptions from active military service. Judge Battle distinguished between a bonded exempt and other exempts who were under no obligation to provide any service and were, therefore, eligible for service in the militia or home guard. Judges Battle and Pearson concurred in the decision to discharge the petitioner. Judge Manly's dissenting opinion reviewed the law; the position was taken that there was nothing more than a contractual obligation to furnish supplies. Failure to fulfill the obligation would mean liability on the part of the obligor on both the bond and for damages. Manly reasoned that a person could pursue his occupation and still be a part of the home guard, and he felt that the petitioner should be ordered into such service.[72]

Commenting on the call for detailed men, including those who had given bond to furnish provisions, the *Standard* stated:

To say nothing of this palpable breach of faith towards the bonded men, this order placing in service all detailed men, and the State order placing the Home Guard in the field, will cause the loss of a large quantity of corn, peas, potatoes, and the like, and will prevent the seeding of thousands of acres of wheat. We cannot hope to cope with the enemy in numbers. We should look rather to strategy and rapid fighting. If *all* the able bodied farmers and mechanics are taken away and put in the army, the country must, sooner or later, become a desolation. But it is useless to protest, or to argue with those who have the control of public affairs.[73]

Other cases were also heard involving home guard problems. For example, mail carriers sought exemption from the guard on the ground that they were civil officers. One David L. Bringle had a contract to carry the mail from Concord to Mill Hill, a distance of eighteen miles; he claimed exemption on the contention that he was a civil officer. A writ of certiorari took the case to the Supreme Court, where Judge Battle found that the petitioner's duties with regard to the mail were incompatible with service in the home guard. He pointed out the legal provisions of the home guard act, showing that civil and military officers of the Confederacy were exempted. Based on its finding that a mail contractor was to be deemed a civil officer, the Court granted the discharge to Bringle.[74]

[72] T. S. Wood v. John A. Bradshaw, 60 N.C. 420 (1864), and record in Original Supreme Court Papers. See also Gavin H. Clark *et al.* v. W. A. Pearson, a Halifax County case, 1864, in Original Supreme Court Papers.

[73] Raleigh *Standard*, October 19, 1864.

[74] David L. Bringle v. John A. Bradshaw, 60 N.C. 514 (1864), and record in Original Supreme Court Papers. See Marcellus Jordan v. James R. Cole, 1864, in Guilford County Papers, a case in which Judge Pearson reached the same conclusion on similar facts.

Persons from other jurisdictions, even foreign countries, could not escape entanglement with the conscription laws. A citizen of Maryland who had been born in North Carolina but who had lived in Maryland for years returned to his home state because of the war and the "consequence of sentiments in favor of the South, expressed by him publicly in the city of Baltimore, . . . [which made it become] necessary for his safety for him to depart that State and come South. . . ." Though he intended to return to Maryland and had exercised no privileges of citizenship in North Carolina, the petitioner suddenly found himself arrested by the enrolling officer. Judge Pearson issued a writ of habeas corpus, heard the case, and decided that the man had no intention of abandoning his Maryland domicile. As a consequence of his reasoning, Judge Pearson discharged the man.[75]

Natives of Scotland and Germany did not have the success of the Marylander, for two petitioners were remanded to the custody of the enrolling officers after their legal efforts failed. The Scot had gone to North Carolina in 1847, with the intention of visiting his mother. The woman had persuaded him to stay for her lifetime, but he claimed he was "now and always has been a subject of her Britannic Majesty, Queen Victoria. . . ." The British Consulate in Charleston, South Carolina, filed an affidavit to the effect that the man was a British subject. Copies of documents pertaining to the liability of British subjects with regard to military duty were introduced as evidence. President Davis was quoted as saying that treaties made by the United States before the separation of the Confederacy were binding on the new country, except where foreign nations had refused the Confederate States the benefit of treaties. The assumption was that rights thereby obtained by individuals were to be recognized. Superior Court Judge Robert R. Heath, in January, 1865, decided that the petitioner, who had been in the country since 1847 and who had exercised the right of suffrage at least once, was a domiciled foreigner subject to military service. He ruled that the arguments advanced in the man's behalf were invalid.[76]

A native of Bavaria, who came to the United States in 1860, was not naturalized and had no intention of changing his domicile; but he was arrested by the enrolling officer under the act of February 17, 1864. Facts showed that the Bavarian owned a home and land as well as a "large & flourishing tan-yard. . . ." He had, in the summer of 1862, gone to a camp of instruction, enrolled, and been exempted for physical disability. After that time he had presented himself regularly for enrollment and examination. The military officers stated that he had not claimed to be a citizen of Germany until the late date of 1865 "when every other possible Shift and Contrivance to avoid the service of his

[75] In the Matter of Dudley Nichols, 1864, in Guilford County Papers.
[76] In the Matter of Daniel McGill, 1865, in Cumberland County Papers.

Country have utterly failed." Judge Pearson, on February 13, 1865, found that the man had gained domicile in North Carolina and was a resident within the meaning of the conscription laws, even though he had never been naturalized. The record shows that the man procured another writ in Richmond, but he was again remanded, in March, 1865.[77]

Because of its desperate plight, the Confederacy was drawing on all available men. Not only foreigners but even Negroes were included; and even before the law relating to the use of Negroes was amended in February,[78] an order called for the enrollment of male slaves between the ages of twelve and fifty for work on fortifications.[79] Attempts were also made to include free Negroes in the enlarged sources of men for the army.

These attempts, too, resulted in judicial interpretation. One James Casey, of Haywood County, a free Negro, had conveyed his services to James R. Love for ninety-nine years by means of a deed. About September 14, 1864, Casey was ordered to report as a conscript free Negro, and he did so. Facts showed that Love had died, but the services of Casey were claimed by Love's executors. Petitioning for a writ of habeas corpus, the Negro was turned down by Judge E. G. Reade in Waynesville. He then appealed to the Supreme Court, asking for a review of the Congressional act which made all male free Negroes between eighteen and fifty years of age liable for the performance of such duties as the Secretary of War should prescribe. The law provided that these men were to be paid eleven dollars a month, receive rations, and be given clothing.

The government did not proceed against Casey as a slave, who could be impressed, but as a free Negro. It was ironic that a former slave should base his argument on the contention that he was not a free Negro but one who had been degraded from that status to a condition of servitude by his deed to Love. The Court ruled that there could be no middle ground—that a man was either free and within the provisions of the act of February 17 or a slave who could not sue and was, therefore, out of court—and concluded that the deed did not remove Casey from the classification of free Negro. The determination was made that free Negroes could be used for specified duties under authority given to the War Department to place such men where they were needed and where they could best serve. The Supreme Court held that Congress was within its rights in providing for the service of such persons in consideration of the society of the Confederacy and in consideration of

[77] In the Matter of Karl Kahnweiler, 1865, in Guilford County Papers.

[78] *Confederate Laws*, 1 Cong., 4 Sess., 1863-1864, c. LXXIX. This section is discussed on page 64.

[79] William F. Foushee to Marmaduke S. Robins, citing order from Adjutant General of North Carolina, January 8, 1864, in Robins Papers.

other legislation regarding the Negro race. The petitioner was, as a consequence of the decision, remanded to the custody of the military authorities.[80] Several similar cases were decided in the same way.[81]

In its eagerness to conscript as many as possible, steps were taken to enroll some members of religious sects which had been exempted by a June amendment to the act of February 17. The amendment gave the Secretary of War authority to exempt members of denominations mentioned in the act of October 11, 1862, provided the persons desiring exemption were members of those particular sects at the time the original act became law.[82] Even after passage of the amendment, some members of the exempted groups had conscription problems. A letter from Camp Holmes was written to Marmaduke Robins in the fall of 1864, in which the writer said:

> I want to now whether thee will under take to git me off from this place I Joind the friends in 62 and in 63 I pade five hundred dollers to the guverment for my Exemption as a friend I would like to now whether the guvernmente has a rite to me and my money two I would like to now what the would charg me to see into my Case and try to git A Discharge for me I will binde my self to let the guvernmente have all the produse tha I can spare at governmente prise if they will releas me for for [sic] further infurmation inquire of E H Strawn Sineter from Chattian I want thee to write to me and let me now whether thee will under take for me I remane thy friend until death Jesse D. Buckner[83]

Others with religious scruples appealed to the courts. A minister of the Methodist Episcopal Church, South, petitioned for release under the provision of the act of February 17 which granted exemptions to ministers authorized to preach according to the rules of their churches and regularly employed in ministerial duties. The commandant of conscripts argued that the Bureau of Conscription's regulations provided that a person who had his ministerial duties for his sole business was entitled to exemption, but that a man who relied on another source of support, even if he did preach regularly, was not so entitled. Judge Battle raised the question of the right of the Bureau to make regulations supplementary to the law; he proceeded to answer his question in the negative. Determining that lack of payment for services was not equivalent to a negation of his usefulness and productiveness in those services, Judge Battle decided in the petitioner's favor and discharged him.[84]

[80] James Casey v. L. S. Robards, 60 N.C. 434 (1864), and in Original Supreme Court Papers.

[81] In the Matter of George Casey, 1864, and In the Matter of Richard Gray, 1864, both Haywood County cases, in Original Supreme Court Papers.

[82] *Confederate Laws*, 2 Cong., 1 Sess., 1864, c. XXIV.

[83] Jesse D. Buckner to Marmaduke Robins, November 24, 1864, in Robins Papers.

[84] In the Matter of William H. Cunninggim, 60 N.C. 392 (1864).

The provision of the February law which created the greatest amount of controversy was undoubtedly that portion providing for the exemption of officials necessary for the administration of state government. The leading case, so far as resultant discussion and correspondence between state and Confederate officials was concerned, involved a man later to serve as Governor of North Carolina, Daniel L. Russell, Jr. Russell was elected a county commissioner in Brunswick County, with the duty assigned to him of distributing allotments to wives and children of soldiers.   In March, 1864, he was threatened with arrest as a conscript, at which time he appealed to Governor Vance.   Vance claimed him as an officer of the state.   When Russell continued his duties as commissioner, he was ordered to camp.   He then applied to Judge Pearson for a writ of habeas corpus, which was granted on July 13, 1864.   The return of Major General W. H. C. Whiting showed that Russell was, on January 20 of that year, a captain of Company G, 36th Regiment, that he had been tried by a general court-martial in February, 1864, and that the sentence had been approved by Whiting so far as deprivation of his commission was concerned.   Russell was given the privilege of selecting another company and was granted a thirty-day leave to make application in Richmond for a change of the sentence.

The act of February 17, in conjunction with General Orders Number 24, provided that officers dropped from the rolls were to be enrolled. Whiting argued that Russell was about nineteen years of age and his infancy prevented him from holding the office of county commissioner; he argued further that the petitioner had never been discharged from service.   At the time he issued his return, Whiting was unaware of the whereabouts of Russell, saying he was away without leave.[85]

Judge Pearson ruled that the question of whether or not Russell was still in service was beside the point in that the real question to be determined was concerned with an exemption granted to a person in service at the time of his election or appointment to state office. Pearson indicated that the appointment did indeed exempt a person from military service, by the Constitution, by the act of Congress, and by the certificate of the Governor.   The government's authority to raise armies was subject to various restrictions, including those which provided for the exemption of necessary state officers.   State legislatures were given power to decide which officers were needed, and county commissioners had been designated as essential in North Carolina.   As there was no Constitutional provision saying a man could not go from service into a state office, such a man would become exempt upon certification by the Governor.   The Chief Justice felt that the question of Russell's qualifi-

[85] In the Matter of D. L. Russell, 60 N.C. 388 (1864), and record in Original Supreme Court Papers. See also numerous letters, record of court-martial, and other pertinent documents in Daniel Lindsey Russell Papers, Southern Historical Collection, University of North Carolina. (Hereinafter cited as Russell Papers.)

cation for office, so far as his age was concerned, was one which could not be attacked collaterally; the validity of the appointment could only be questioned in another proceeding. Again, Pearson stressed his feeling that the act suspending the writ of habeas corpus was inapplicable in the Russell case because it was the intention of Congress to suspend the writ only in criminal matters. Russell, therefore, received a discharge.[86]

Russell's case was the subject of extensive correspondence, both before and after Judge Pearson handed down his decision. Secretary of War Seddon had written to Governor Vance on May 2, 1864, referring to correspondence between the Governor and Whiting relative to the exemption of Russell. Seddon pointed out that there was no act of Congress providing for the discharge of a person belonging to the army merely because of his election to a state office, and that the only exception was that in the act of April 2, 1863, dealing with the election of senators and representatives in Congress and state legislatures, judges, and other high officials. He explained that a person claiming the exemption had to be outside the army, whereas Russell was in service in February when the act was passed. At the date of the passage of the law, Russell was not a county official because he had obtained that position later. Seddon concluded by saying that the matter had been considered before, and after regulations of the War Department had been explained, its decisions had been followed.[87]

Governor Vance discussed the Russell case at length in a letter to Seddon, saying he felt the exemption of state officers to be independent of Congressional action. Vance took the position that Russell was not in service when he was elected a commissioner. After presenting his arguments, the Governor had concluded by saying, "Should I be in error upon the law of the case, I must earnestly urge upon you not to wound the spirit of this gallant and promising young officer by sending him into the ranks."[88] In July, he wrote to Whiting to say he had had no reply to his letter concerning Russell, that he understood Russell had been ordered to camp, and that he would not submit to the order without resisting such action, "especially in favor of a government that will not answer a respectful letter on the subject." He continued by averring that an order to arrest Russell would be considered "a deliberate & unwarranted usurpation of authority. . . ."[89]

Seddon then replied that the reasoning of Vance would mean that the North Carolina General Assembly could withdraw all of the state's troops for service within the state. "The Department has conceded

[86] In the Matter of D. L. Russell, 60 N.C. 388 (1864).
[87] James A. Seddon to Zebulon B. Vance, May 2, 1864, in *Official Records*, Series IV, III, 375.
[88] Vance to Seddon, May 19, 1864, in Russell Papers.
[89] Zebulon B. Vance to W. H. C. Whiting, July 5, 1864, in Russell Papers.

many things to the government of North Carolina with the view to secure a cordial co-operation of the government . . . but it cannot make a concession of a principle so vital as the one contained in the question under discussion."[90] Seddon wrote to Whiting the same day to suggest that if Whiting arrested Russell and took him into custody, he should make a return to any writ and indicate that he was holding Russell under the law suspending the writ of habeas corpus for seeking to evade military service.[91]

The decision of Judge Pearson was handed down on July 25, 1864.[92] Russell, having heard of an order for his arrest, wrote to Major General Whiting on August 7, saying he had been discharged by the Chief Justice on a writ of habeas corpus, and also informing the military authorities of his election as a delegate to the General Assembly from Brunswick County. He requested a passport for a period of thirty or sixty days so that he could discharge his duties without interference.[93] In his reply, Whiting stated that he did not acknowledge either the claim of the Governor or the decision of the Chief Justice, but he admitted that election to the General Assembly complicated the question. He promised to refer the new angle to the War Department for instructions, and he assured Russell that he would not be molested prior to a decision from that Department.[94]

Because of a newspaper report in which the Russell decision had been carried Russell wrote to the editor, summarizing step-by-step the case, beginning with an explanation of the circumstances leading to his arrest and subsequent court-martial.[95] At length, the case was ended when Special Orders Number 309, dated December 30, 1864, and sent to Russell through General Lee, informed the subject of this extensive correspondence that President Davis had remitted the sentence of dismissal imposed by the court-martial in February, 1864, and that Russell was thereby being restored to duty with his command.[96]

Though Judge Pearson's decision in the Russell case was later overruled by the full Supreme Court,[97] it was cited repeatedly. Judge Battle referred to it in discharging a petitioner, though he reserved

[90] James A. Seddon to Zebulon B. Vance, July 23, 1864, in *Official Records*, Series IV, III, 555-556.

[91] James A. Seddon to W. H. C. Whiting, July 23, 1864, in *Official Records*, Series IV, III, 556.

[92] See note following case of In the Matter of D. L. Russell, 60 N.C. 388 (1864).

[93] Daniel L. Russell to W. H. C. Whiting, August 7, 1864, in Russell Papers.

[94] Whiting to Russell, August 11, 1864, in Russell Papers.

[95] Daniel L. Russell to Editor, Raleigh *Conservative*, August 11, 1864, in Russell Papers.

[96] Special Orders No. 309, December 30, 1864, signed by H. L. Clay, Assistant Adjutant General, in Russell Papers.

[97] See note following case of In the Matter of D. L. Russell, 60 N.C. 388 (1864).

the right to change his mind when the case went before the entire Court for review. In the opinion written on behalf of the Supreme Court after the case had been heard on appeal, Judge Battle did change his opinion. He reviewed the various conscription provisions and concluded that Congress did not intend to release soldiers in service by the act of February. He discussed the respective powers of the Confederate and the state governments. In his reasoning, Judge Battle stated that the Confederacy had no power to destroy state governments; as a consequence, the government of the Confederate States did not have authority to conscript officers necessary to the operation of state government. On the other hand, Judge Battle found that the state was not permitted to remove from Confederate service a man already there by electing him to state office. In answer to the argument that an equally qualified man could not be found for the office, Battle pointed out the logical conclusion that the Confederacy could not find an equally qualified man as a soldier. Judge Manly concurred with Judge Battle in his decision that his own early opinion, rendered in vacation, was erroneous. Following his consistent course, Judge Pearson dissented.[98]

The Battle decision was cited as a precedent in another case involving a boy appointed by his father, the sheriff, to be his deputy. Evidence showed that the boy had been enrolled in the junior reserves when he reached the age of seventeen on October 7, 1863. The next September, during the period the boy was home on furlough, the father deputized his son and the soldier failed to return to the army when his furlough expired. Judge Battle determined that the boy was in the military service at the time of his appointment and was not within the exemption provisions; the petitioner was remanded.[99]

Variations in decisions often resulted from slight differences in facts presented to the judges. A man named William D. Johnson had been elected to the police force in Raleigh in January, 1864. He was assigned the duty of keeping the city pumps in order. Evidence showed that Johnson was regarded by the board of commissioners as a policeman, that he had been required to perform police duties from time to time over a period of months, and that keeping the pumps in order was considered a police function. Judge Battle held that the evidence was sufficient to support the position that the petitioner was a policeman, but the question at issue was whether or not he was entitled to exemption. Referring to a Virginia Court of Appeals decision in which the court had found that Congress had no power to order conscription of state officers and that the act of February 17 had provided that the governors of the several states should say which officers were necessary for their states, Battle declared that the petitioner had not relied on a certificate from the Governor but rather on an act of the General As-

[98] Seth Bridgman v. Peter Mallett, 60 N.C. 500 (1864).
[99] Samuel R. Philpot v. John S. Price, 1864, in Original Supreme Court Papers.

sembly. That act, which provided that specified officers were essential, had included the mayor and police of the city of Raleigh. After raising the question of the right of the legislature to make such provisions, Judge Battle answered that it could do so and that it could also appoint the Governor as its agent to certify its decisions. Judges Battle and Pearson concurred in the decision to exempt Johnson.[100]

A significant case in that it was one of those overruling the Russell decision was that of Robert H. Smith of Salisbury, a man who had employed a substitute before he was later called into service. While proceedings were suspended in his petition for a writ of habeas corpus, pending a Supreme Court decision in the Walton case, Smith was appointed a watchman or policeman for the town of Salisbury. On May 23, 1864, he appeared before the enrolling officer and asked for exemption. Judge Pearson, in chambers, held that the petitioner was taken out of the custody of the military authorities, but the case went to the full Supreme Court on a writ of certiorari. Judge Manly's opinion stated that Smith was enrolled prior to his appointment as a watchman and had been put in military service. His status was not that of a state officer, but "is as firmly fixed as if he were in the trenches, confronting the enemy." Smith was remanded to the military authorities.[101] A similar case involving another policeman was decided in the same way.[102]

The situation with regard to state officers was far from clear. There were conflicting statements both in correspondence and in legal opinions. Early in November, Governor Vance wrote to General T. H. Holmes, commenting that he was conforming to the request for the list of classes of persons he had claimed as being essential to state government. He referred to Johnson v. Mallett in which the North Carolina Supreme Court had stated that the Governor's certificate in behalf of an officer was not material. He did indicate that offices would be filled by nonconscripts insofar as possible. The letter was forwarded to the Bureau of Conscription by Holmes and from there to the Secretary of War. An endorsement, initialed by the Secretary, asked the Assistant Secretary, J. A. Campbell, whether he had seen or heard of the decision mentioned therein. He also asked whether or not he was bound to act upon the conscript law without reference to the state decisions, pointing out the conflicting results which would ensue should the decisions be followed. The Assistant Secretary replied that he had not seen the decision, but that it corresponded with one made by Chief Justice Pear-

[100] William D. Johnson v. Peter Mallett, 60 N.C. 410 (1864), and record filed in Original Supreme Court Papers.

[101] Robert H. Smith v. John N. Prior, 60 N.C. 417 (1864), and record filed in Original Supreme Court Papers.

[102] In the Matter of William R. Clark, 1864, in Original Supreme Court Papers.

son "in the case of one Russell (I think that is the name), who was conscribed by General Whiting. Governor Vance presses the decision beyond its limits when he claims all the employes and agents, &c. The decision, in my opinion, is erroneous, as militating against that supremacy which the Constitution ordains in respect to the legislation of the Confederate States in the subjects committed to them."[103]

The military officers were seemingly fighting a losing battle with the courts. Legal procedures caused delay even when the petitioners were remanded to the military personnel. A report of inspection at Camp Holmes, in June, 1864, showed that there were numerous problems. Colonel Mallett had too small a guard to prevent conscripts from escaping, and he could not furnish a traveling guard for those conscripts sent to various armies.[104] The number of applications for detail were almost as numerous as the number of men enrolled;[105] and petitions were used to cause delay, resulting in numbers of conscripts spending "a quiet summer at home by means of a petition."[106]

The public tended to feel that the matter of exemptions worked unequally and depended to a large extent on "the partiality of those in whose hands is placed the execution of them."[107]

Figures submitted to Secretary of War J. C. Breckinridge in February, 1865, indicated that North Carolina had enrolled and sent to camps of instruction after the passage of the act of April 16, 1862, a total of 21,348 men out of 81,993 in nine states. North Carolina had furnished 8,000 out of over 72,000 who had joined the army without going through a camp of instruction. Exemptions from North Carolina had included 7,885 physically disabled; 69 officers of the Confederacy; 5,589 state officers; 400 ministers; five superintendents and physicians of institutions for the deaf, dumb, and blind; 21 editors and 99 newspaper employees; 31 apothecaries; 374 physicians; 173 teachers; 246 overseers and agriculturalists; 967 railroad people; 100 mail contractors and 47 drivers of post coaches and hacks; 342 non-combatants; 167 foreigners; 49 persons exempted by orders of the War Department, making a total of 16,564. The grand total for Virginia, North Carolina, South Carolina, Georgia, Alabama, Mississippi, Florida, East Tennessee, and East Louisiana was 67,054.[108] In addition to those

[103] Zebulon B. Vance to T. H. Holmes, November 2, 1864, in *Official Records*, Series IV, III, 754-755, and endorsements on letter, p. 755.
[104] Report of Inspection of Camp Holmes, June 16, 1864, by Archer Anderson, in *Official Records*, Series IV, III, 490.
[105] Archer Anderson to Braxton Bragg, June 22, 1864, in *Official Records*, Series IV, III, 504-506.
[106] Anderson to Bragg, July 18, 1864, in *Official Records*, Series IV, III, 539-542.
[107] Raleigh *Standard*, January 4, 1865, quoting the Richmond *Whig*. See also Douglas, "Conscription," p. 14.
[108] Figures submitted by John S. Preston to J. C. Breckinridge, February, 1865, in *Official Records*, Series IV, III, 1101-1102.

exempted in North Carolina, there were 229 agricultural details; 437 details for public necessity, including tanners, millers, factory workers and other such laborers; 717 details of contractors to furnish supplies; and 1,885 details in the category of artisans, including such groups as persons affiliated with the postal, navy, medical, and treasury departments.[109]

A report on the operation of the conscription act from January 1 to April 1, 1864, indicated that the source of men was nearly exhausted and that the act of January 5, ending the exemption of those who had furnished substitutes, had not provided the number desired. Many with substitutes were within other exemptions provided by sections of the act of February 17; some were subject to detail. The report contained a note of defeat in stating "that there seems to have been a general effort to keep principals of substitutes out of the Army."[110]

In November, John S. Preston told of the difficulty in obtaining accurate information. He wrote:

It is well known that the laws of North Carolina have created large numbers of officers, and that the Governor of that State has not only claimed exemption for those officers, but for all persons employed in any form by the State of North Carolina, such as workmen in factories, salt makers, &c. This Bureau has no power to enforce the Confederate law in opposition to the Governor's certificates or the claims of a State.[111]

Preston indicated a few days earlier that North Carolina had exempted 14,675 state officers out of a total for nine states of 18,843,[112] but this report was probably not so accurate as that made in February when the number was shown as 5,589.[113]

The over-all situation—a dark picture—was presented in a report sent to Secretary of War J. C. Breckinridge by John A. Campbell, the Assistant Secretary, and dated March 5, 1865. He stated that second in importance to finances, and perhaps equally important, was the question of the condition of the armies. Reviewing the various acts of Congress with regard to conscription, beginning in April, 1862, and going on through the stringent law of February, 1864, Campbell summarized the several Congressional provisions. He referred to the large number of casualties which the Confederate armies had sustained, and he observed that replacements could not be made from conscripts.

[109] See tables giving statistical information, in *Official Records*, Series IV, III, 1104-1109.

[110] John S. Preston to James A. Seddon, April 30, 1864, in *Official Records*, Series IV, III, 354-355.

[111] Preston to Seddon, November 29, 1864, in *Official Records*, Series IV, III, 866-867.

[112] Preston to Seddon, November 23, 1864, in *Official Records*, Series IV, III, 851.

[113] Douglas, "Conscription," pp. 27-28.

Mentioning the fact that there were over 100,000 deserters in the Confederacy, he suggested that escape was so common that no stigma resulted. North Carolina, South Carolina, Georgia, and perhaps other states had laws withdrawing from service men considered by the Confederate authorities to be subject thereto; these laws had local support, according to Campbell's understanding. Attempts to recruit twenty thousand men had been obstructed, and "The enemy have raised about as many from the fugitives occasioned by the draft as ourselves from its execution. General Holmes reports 1500 fugitives in one week in North Carolina." The low morale, lack of subsistence for the men, and similar problems were mentioned in the concluding paragraphs of the report.[114]

Problems which plagued the Confederacy also troubled the Union. In the North there were many judges who denied the validity of the suspension of the writ of habeas corpus when such a step was taken to invoke military control over civilians. Powers assumed by President Abraham Lincoln were far-reaching and could easily be interpreted as dictatorial in more than one instance.[115] The constitutionality of conscription in the North was never tested, but the law would undoubtedly have been upheld had it gone to the United States Supreme Court for review. There were opponents in the North who argued that the states' rights position was correct and should be applied. The preponderance of legal opinion in the North upheld the validity of legislation passed to make the military forces effective.[116]

Despite problems, conflicts, and hardships on both sides, the legal questions continued to be heard. Throughout the months and years of the conflict, Judge Richmond M. Pearson had conscientiously upheld what he believed to be the "fundamental principles of constitutional freedom [which] were disregarded...." He listened to many citizens of North Carolina "who fled to the civil courts for refuge from the oppressions of military power."[117] Judge Matthias E. Manly was prevented by illness from participating in many of the habeas corpus cases taken to the Supreme Court in 1863, but he was present in 1864. He tended to uphold the right of the Confederacy to the services of its citizens.[118] Judge William H. Battle, the third member of the highest tribunal of North Carolina, was more unpredictable than his colleagues, maintaining an independent course.[119] Despite their differences of judicial interpretation and conclusions, a sufficient number of legal de-

[114] John A. Campbell to J. C. Breckinridge, March 5, 1865, typed copy in Campbell-Colston Papers, Southern Historical Collection, University of North Carolina.

[115] Randall, *Constitutional Problems*, pp. 120, 183.

[116] *Ibid.*, pp. 268-274.

[117] Dick, "Richmond M. Pearson," V, 303.

[118] Ashe, "Matthias E. Manly," VI, 360.

[119] Ashe, "William H. Battle," VI, 22.

cisions favoring petitioners bringing suits for writs of habeas corpus were handed down to obstruct the military authorities in their endeavors. Public opinion, which in many areas of North Carolina was opposed to conscription, found support in judicial opinions.

The influence of the North Carolina Supreme Court on the course of the Civil War, not only in North Carolina but throughout the Confederacy, is more vital than is generally realized. A study of the opinions, both reported and not reported, reveal much about attitudes, opinions, desires, and actions of men called upon to defend their newly-formed country. The lack of whole-hearted support is apparent throughout the legal opinions, and the backing by the Court of many citizens who appealed to its judges to support citizens in their thinking makes clearly evident the weakness of the Confederacy as a government. The fact that the highest court of one state could cause dismay, grief, and actual losses to the Confederacy is, in itself, indicative of the character of the central government formed in 1861. The obvious weaknesses are outstanding when the legal opinions are studied. The failure of the Confederacy to set up a federal court of appeals in which state decisions could be reviewed was an inherent defect which contributed to the downfall of that government.

A mere reading of the statutes passed by the several sessions of the Confederate Congress reflects the trend of the war. The judicial interpretation given to the conscription and exemption laws by judges of the Superior and Supreme courts in North Carolina added to the confusion, discontent, and chaos which existed in the Confederacy. Enforcement of the exemption provisions weakened a link in the chain needed for a strong, united fighting force. The constant battle between the civil courts and the military authorities proved to be a major factor leading to a breakdown of military might and the ultimate surrender of the Confederate forces in April, 1865. The lack of legal support for military action was not the sole cause for defeat by any means, but the nonexistence of co-operation and of support from North Carolina and other state governments played a major role in the disastrous defeat of the Confederacy. One can only wonder what the outcome would have been had the Confederate government been backed in its plans and actions by a strong judiciary, both on the state level and as part of the central government. A changed attitude on the part of the judges of the South might have done much to have helped maintain the spirit of unity and enthusiasm with which citizens greeted news of secession and war in 1861. But speculation is futile; facts stand; the legal system was one of many weak links in the Confederate chain, and the outcome, disastrous for the South at the time, proved to be the salvation of citizens of North and South as the years of the war passed into the background and the future of the United States assumed new and great proportions for all the people.

BIBLIOGRAPHY

I Primary Sources

A Manuscripts

Campbell-Colston Papers, 1781, 1855-1920. 670 items. Collection includes papers and correspondence of John A. Campbell, Assistant Secretary of War of the Confederate States. Southern Historical Collection, University of North Carolina.

Chatham County Confederate Papers, 1861-1865, 1885. Included in collection are records of varied descriptions from Chatham County; Civil War court cases among the papers. Archives, State Department of Archives and History, Raleigh.

Cumberland County Miscellaneous Court Records, 1817-1878. Collection includes numerous cases relating to the Civil War. Archives, State Department of Archives and History, Raleigh.

Davidson County Miscellaneous County Records, 1823-1922. Civil War records filed in collection. Archives, State Department of Archives and History, Raleigh.

Guilford County Miscellaneous Papers, 1799-1868. Civil War court records included in collection. Archives, State Department of Archives and History, Raleigh.

Peter Mallett Papers, 1785-1913. Approximately 1,200 items. Mallett's role as Commandant of the North Carolina Bureau of Conscription is reflected in this collection. Southern Historical Collection, University of North Carolina.

Richmond M. Pearson Papers, 1816-1878. 350 items. As the key judicial figure in the interpretation of the conscription and exemption laws, the paucity of papers on this particular question and period is disappointing. Southern Historical Collection, University of North Carolina.

Marmaduke Robins Papers, 1825-1887. 440 items. As private secretary to Governor Vance, the papers of Robins add much to a study of conscription problems. Southern Historical Collection, University of North Carolina.

Daniel Lindsay Russell Papers, 1839-1910. 1,984 items. Russell, later Governor of North Carolina, was embroiled in the conflict between the military authorities and the courts. The papers contain much of interest on this matter. Southern Historical Collection, University of North Carolina.

Secretary of State's Papers, Constitutional Convention, 1861-

1862. Archives, State Department of Archives and History, Raleigh.

Original Records of the North Carolina Supreme Court, late 1700's to the present. The original transcripts, complaints, answers, depositions, briefs, opinions, and related legal documents pertaining to cases on appeal are included in these records. The original records and the printed reports vary in that some of the cases were not reported and there is no published opinion; on the other hand, no original records were found for some of the published cases. Some of the records contain a wealth of material while others are incomplete. These records were folded and tied in bundles years ago; the job of arranging them properly, microfilming them, and refiling them was begun in 1958 by the State Department of Archives and History. The records for the war years were used in this study, but a few documents pertaining to the Civil War were found in cases appealed after 1865. Original records filed in office of the Clerk of the North Carolina Supreme Court, Raleigh.

University of North Carolina Papers, 1770-1936. Approximately 60,000 items. A letter or two relating to problems resulting from the Civil War included in collection. Southern Historical Collection, University of North Carolina at Chapel Hill.

B Official Documents

Commager, Henry Steele, ed., "The Constitution of the Confederate States of America," *Documents of American History*. Third Edition (New York: F. S. Crofts and Co., 1944), pp. 376-384.

Confederate States of America *Public Acts of the Provisional Congress*, 5 sessions, 1861-1862.

Confederate States of America *Public Laws*, 1-2 Congresses, 1862-1864.

Confederate States of America *House Journal*, 1861-1865.

Confederate States of America *Senate Journal*, 1861-1865.

Ordinances of the State Convention (North Carolina), 4 sessions, 1861-1862.

North Carolina *Public Laws*, 1861-1865.

North Carolina *House Journal*, 1861.

North Carolina *Senate Journal*, 1861.

North Carolina *Supreme Court Reports*, 1861-1864, 1869. Volumes 53, 60, and 63.

Resolutions of a Public Nature (North Carolina), 1862-1863.

C Newspapers

Carolina Watchman (Weekly), Salisbury, 1861-1864.
North-Carolina Weekly Standard, Raleigh, 1861-1865.
North Carolina Whig, Charlotte, 1862.
Semi-Weekly Raleigh Register, 1861-1862.
Weekly Raleigh Register, 1861, 1863.

D Memoirs, Correspondence, and Published Records

Clark, Walter, ed., *The State Records of North Carolina*, 16 volumes and 4-volume index (compiled by Stephen B. Weeks for both *Colonial Records* and *State Records*). Winston, Goldsboro, Raleigh: The State of North Carolina, 1895-1914.

Scott, R. N. *et al.*, eds., *The War of the Rebellion: A Compilation of the Official Records of the Union and Confederate Armies*, 70 volumes in 127 books, atlases, and index. Washington: Government Printing Office, 1880-1901.

Shotwell, Randolph Abbott, *The Papers of...*, 2 volumes. Edited by J. G. de Roulhac Hamilton with the collaboration of Rebecca Cameron. Raleigh: The North Carolina Historical Commission, 1929-1936.

Vance, Zebulon Baird, *The Papers of...*, 1 volume of projected series. Edited by Frontis W. Johnston. Raleigh: State Department of Archives and History, 1963.

Worth, Jonathan, *The Correspondence of...*, 2 volumes. Edited by J. G. de Roulhac Hamilton. Raleigh: The North Carolina Historical Commission, 1909.

II Secondary Sources

A General Works

Barrett, John G., *The Civil War in North Carolina*. Chapel Hill: The University of North Carolina Press, c. 1963.

Crabtree, Beth G., *North Carolina Governors, 1585-1958: Brief Sketches*. Raleigh: State Department of Archives and History, 1958.

Hyman, Harold Melvin, *Era of the Oath: Northern Loyalty Tests During the Civil War and Reconstruction*. Philadelphia: University of Pennsylvania Press, 1954.

Lefler, Hugh Talmage and Albert Ray Newsome, *The History of a Southern State: North Carolina*. Revised Edition. Chapel Hill: The University of North Carolina Press, c. 1963.

King, Spender Bidwell, Jr., *Selective Service in North Carolina in World War II*. Chapel Hill: The University of North Carolina Press, 1949.

Lonn, Ella, *Desertion During the Civil War*. New York: Century Company, c. 1928.

Moore, Albert Burton, *Conscription and Conflict in the Confederacy*. New York: Hillary House Publishers Ltd. (Reprint of 1924 publication of The Macmillan Company), 1963.

Randall, J. G. and David Donald, *The Divided Union*. Boston and Toronto: Little, Brown and Company, c. 1961.

Randall, James G., *Constitutional Problems Under Lincoln*. New York and London: D. Appleton and Company, 1926.

Wright, Edward Needles, *Conscientious Objectors in the Civil War*. New York: A. S. Barnes and Company, Inc. (Reprint of 1931 publication of University of Pennsylvania Press), 1961.

B Biographical Sketches, Articles, and Special Studies

Ashe, S. A., "Matthias Evans Manly," *Biographical History of North Carolina From Colonial Times to the Present*, 8 volumes. Edited by Samuel A. Ashe (Greensboro: Charles L. Van Noppen, 1906-1917), VI, 357-365.

Ashe, S. A., "William Horn Battle," *Biographical History of North Carolina From Colonial Times to the Present*, 8 volumes. Edited by Samuel A. Ashe (Greensboro: Charles L. Van Noppen, 1906-1917), VI, 20-24.

Bardolph, Richard, "Inconstant Rebels: Desertion of North Carolina Troops in the Civil War," *The North Carolina Historical Review*, XLI (Spring, 1964), 163-189.

Douglas, Clarence D., "Conscription and the Writ of Habeas Corpus in North Carolina During the Civil War," *Historical Papers*. (Durham: Trinity College Historical Society, 1922), Series XIV, 5-39.

Dick, Robert P., "Richmond M. Pearson," *Biographical History of North Carolina From Colonial Times to the Present*, 8 volumes. Edited by Samuel A. Ashe (Greensboro: Charles L. Van Noppen, 1906-1917), V, 295-309.

Haywood, Marshall DeLancey, "John Willis Ellis," *Biographical History of North Carolina From Colonial Times to the Present*, 8 volumes. Edited by Samuel A. Ashe (Greensboro: Charles L. Van Noppen, 1906-1917), VII, 94-101.

INDEX